To Tom
From
Pete.

Below Decks:

From pantry boy to steward in the British Merchant Navy, 1954 - 1961

— PETER JOSEPH TROY —

An environmentally friendly book printed and bound in England by
www.printondemand-worldwide.com

This book is made entirely of chain-of-custody materials

FastPrint Publishing

www.fast-print.net/store.php

Below Decks: From pantry boy to steward in the British Merchant Navy, 1954 - 1961
Copyright © Peter Joseph Troy 2013

All rights reserved

No part of this book may be reproduced in any form by photocopying or any electronic or mechanical means, including information storage or retrieval systems, without permission in writing from both the copyright owner and the publisher of the book.

All characters are non-fictional but many names have been changed.

The right of Peter Joseph Troy to be identified as the author of this work has been asserted by him in accordance with the Copyright, Designs and Patents Act 1988 and any subsequent amendments thereto.

A catalogue record for this book is available from the British Library

ISBN 978-178035-672-3

First published 2013 by
FASTPRINT PUBLISHING
Peterborough, England.

Expectations

Expectations are the target in front of me,
Expectations,
Expectations are high,
Long, dark night and the target's in front of me,
Expectations are high,
Long, sleepless night and the target's in front of me,
Expectations are high.
I pick up the bow,
Arrow is drawn,
I shoot too low,
My dreams are torn.
Expectations,
Expectations are high,
I miss my mark,
Nowhere to hide,
I am in the dark,
I shouldn't have tried.
Expectations are high,
Then there is light,
The angel with my hand,
We take off in flight,
To a new land,
Expectations are high.

Levi Farrow (14)
The Ridgeway School & Sixth Form College, Wroughton

Poetry

And the haikus ahead are the prosper in front of me
Poems
Poems
Oh, poetry
Poems
Oh, poetry
Five seven fives are the longing inside of me
Poems
Oh, poetry
Simile
And the poem is ready
Simile
And the sounds still steady
Poems
Oh, poetry
The poems get dark, the words are surrounding me
My poems get dark, the silence is over me
Poems
Oh, poetry
One metaphor
For something to savour
Two metaphors
Just to add some flavour
Poems
Oh, poetry
Add jumbled-up words

Contents

Preface	3
Summer 1954	7
Sea School	19
Maiden Voyage	27
Bellboys, Wingers and Bloods	39
The Panama Canal	57
To the Land of the Long White Cloud	73
Wellington	87
Going South	105
Eight Bob to Battersea	119
A Guest of General Franco	131
Out	153
On the Beach	167
Physical Labour	173
Another Chance	181
To Africa	189
The London Docks: Working By	215
A One Way Trip	223
A Respectable Job	229
The Black & the Chrome	235

Peter Joseph Troy

Winging It   239
Back to Windy Wellington   249
Reflections   255

Preface

Big Eric had warned me not to, but sod you I thought, I'm going and I did – for seven years. That was then, back when I was no more than a kid. Now as an elderly man I reflect on those years and despite the dysfunctional life that followed I wouldn't swap a moment of it – although after returning from my maiden voyage to Canada in the winter of 1955 I seriously considered joining the Army as a lesser form of suffering.

After attending a six-week course at a British Merchant Navy training school on the Bristol Channel I was seventeen and away to sea. I was to spend the next seven years first as a pantry and galley boy, then as a bellboy and finally as a steward. I served aboard cargo vessels, passenger liners and a coal collier back and forth to Tyneside. My old seaman's discharge book reveals that I made twenty-three voyages on a total of sixteen vessels. London-based and free-lance, all I had to do to join a ship was go down to the Pool of London, or maybe to the shipping offices in Leadenhall Street to one of the many major companies, to see what ships were on offer. I could get a ship to any destination that interested me whenever I wanted. I signed articles for

'Home Trade' and 'Deep Sea' and crossed seas and oceans many times. For a child of working-class parents in London, the Merchant Navy offered me – as it did thousands of other young men in the 1950s – not only escape from post-war austerity, but also an exciting lifestyle. We were worked hard, to be sure, but good times were to be had both on board ship and ashore.

Memoirs of service in the British Merchant Navy have been published in the past, but most of these have been written by officers and provide 'the view from the bridge'. I have nothing against officers, but I don't think they are in a position to tell the whole story of the Merchant Navy. Neither am I, but I think my 'view from below decks' will add more balance to the story of an important chapter in Britain's maritime history, not to mention its post-war social history. Aided by my seaman's discharge book, which has jogged my memory of where I went when, and conversations with the fellow shipmates with whom I've kept in contact over the years, I've written with as much candour as I can muster about my experiences both on ship and ashore, the good times as well as the bad. I've invented a few names for people because I can't remember their real names, and I've changed a few other names in order to protect myself.

Some of what follows may provide ammunition for the disdainful view of ordinary sailors and seamen amongst the British public that Tim Madge writes about in his fine book, *Long Voyage Home*. With an advance on our wages on our hips after long weeks at sea, we might well get drunk when we finally got ashore. We could also be 'free and easy' with the local girls, as the old music hall song says. But we were also hard-working (for long hours at fairly low wages), we read the books that the Seamen's Mission made available on British ships in our off hours, and some of us learned more about the world through our travels than was possible at the time for our lubber brethren.

Peter Joseph Troy

Oxford 2013

peterjoetroy@gmail.com

Peter Joseph Troy

Summer 1954

'Merchant Navy!' said Big Eric before lighting a Woodbine. He took a long drag. Then shaking his head from side to side he snorted, 'They're all bent.'

'Bent?' I was puzzled. 'What ya mean, villains?'

'Someone get hold of him and wise him up,' he continued. 'Nancy-boys is what we're on abaht.' He blew smoke down his nose, and those around our table all smirked and looked knowing.

'They can't all be,' I replied, beginning to get his drift. 'And anyhow how can you tell if they are?'

'Well for a start,' he leaned in and lowered his voice, 'you can often tell by their clothes. They all wear yellow dressing gowns and smoke black cigarettes in long holders.' I considered this for a moment but couldn't see my Uncle Jim or Victor's Uncle Snowy wearing a yellow dressing gown, and they'd both been in the Merchant Navy for years. Besides Snowy always smoked Black Cat, and that was only for his throat's sake and never in a cigarette holder.

'And another thing,' said Big Eric just as the work's bell rang, sounding the end of tea break. 'They'll want to be really friendly to a kid like you. Just don't let them show you the golden rivet,' he sniggered. Then draining his cup he stood his full six foot-three and scraped back his chair in one easy movement. 'Come on,' he said and we all followed, drifting out of the canteen and back down to the shop floor.

The idea of going to sea had been in my mind for years; didn't all the nice girls love a sailor? And what about Mum's brothers? The whole family had grown up in Vine Street Buildings beside the Thames in Bermondsey, where City Hall now stands, and three of the boys had gone to sea. With heroic tales of Jutland, Jellicoe and Beatty ringing in their ears since boyhood, two of them – my Uncles Tom and Dick – had become sailors, enlisting in the Royal Navy as soon as they could. But it was my Uncle Jim, who often dodged school to help navigate barges and small craft from the Pool of London down to Gravesend, who became my hero. It wasn't long before he was across the Channel, then up to the Baltic; next heard of he was in Algiers. Mum was in awe of Jim and always had a story to tell.

My favourite was the creepy one. Go on, Mum, tell us, I'd say, and she would but only if my kid sister, Rosie, wasn't present. When we were alone though she'd begin, and each telling of the tale was better than the last.

Below Decks

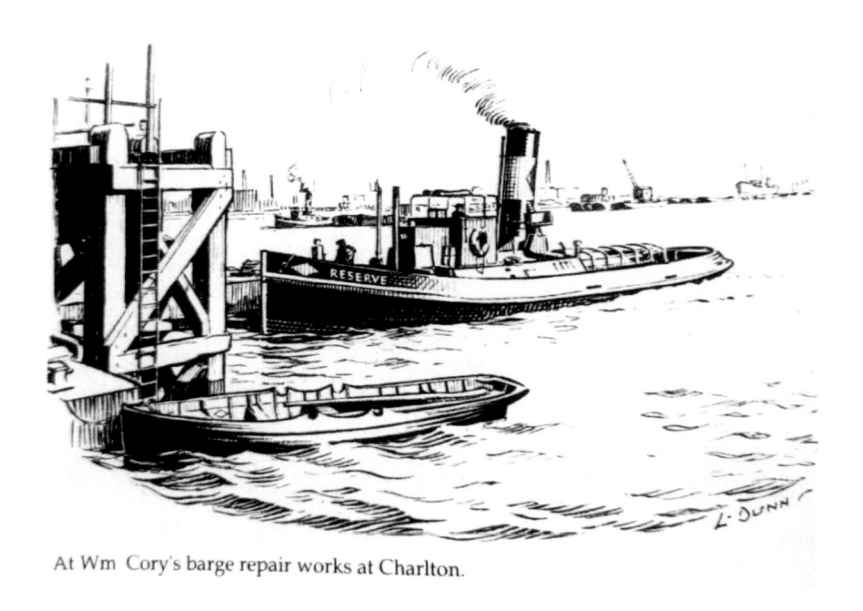

At Wm Cory's barge repair works at Charlton.

'One dark night just off the coast of Venezuela Jim was at the helm. There being no moon and little starlight he had only a faint light from the compass, just enough to steer the ship by. It was sometime during his lonely watch that he became aware he wasn't alone; he felt something was out there in the dark watching him.' It was here she'd pause to give me a moment to be horrified by what I knew was coming. 'To have lit a lamp would have affected his night vision so he didn't, but Jim now began to feel an overpowering tiredness and got the impression that whatever it was out there was the cause. There was something slow and rhythmic, sort of hypnotic, not really a sound but like something large was slowly breathing in and out, waiting out there in the dark.' She'd pause again, and I'd be hanging on her every word. 'Jim was transfixed, couldn't move and knew he would have given in and become its victim. But then the Mate coming up on deck for a pipe, and lighting his

Lucifer, saw what he took for a rook perched upon the rail with its great black wings – slowly rising and falling, wafting Jim to sleep. Too bold to be a rook it turned out to be a large vampire bat and the Mate rushed at it with a broom and drove the creature away.'

'But Mum,' I would remind her, 'what would the bat have done to Uncle Jim had the Mate not rushed at it?'

'Do you really, really want to know?' she would ask in a whisper, and I could only nod my head. 'The bat would have done to Jim what it did to its victims in that part of the world...' It was at this point in her story that the horror of it all would overwhelm me so that I couldn't speak, and she'd conclude with, '...It would have settled at his throat and begun slowly to suck the life-blood from him – *Wooo – Hoooo!*' I would always then get a hug and a kiss from Mum and be reminded of just how interesting my Uncle Jim's experiences were. There it was: foreign lands, adventure and danger.

Besides I had a memory of my own concerning a ship. I remembered being an evacuee in 1941 when Dad accompanied us across the Irish Sea to where his people were, before returning to London to take up his job in munitions and as an air raid warden. The memory was, and still is, remarkable for its clarity. It had been a night passage on a crowded ferry called *The Great Western* from Fishguard to Waterford and although I had been too young to be aware of the dangers of German submarines in the Irish Sea it had been a huge adventure, made all the more exciting by an impression of escaping the Blitz, being on the run to a place of safety.

There'd been the packed steam train from Paddington to the Welsh coast, and then embarkation aboard the vessel, where I'd been sat on Dad's lap and my kid sister, Rosie, on Mum's. We didn't have a berth but sat up all night on the boat deck midst a nervous but jolly Irish crowd, and I'd been hugged against the chill of the night. I had never been up so late or been surrounded by so many grown-ups. There was the smell of pipe tobacco and the clink of bottles. Someone played a squeezebox and another blew a mouth organ whilst others crooned the old songs, Dad joining in between his coughing fits: *'If you ever go across the sea to Ireland...', 'In Dublin's fair city where the girls are so pretty...'* and many more that he'd sung to Rosie and me as lullabies. Nibbling biscuits and cheese and given sips of Dad's Guinness beneath the stars and the salt spray, I'd never felt so protected, precious and loved.

So yes it was always assumed somehow that I'd end up at sea; it was more than an occupation, it was almost a family tradition. Only in the past year, however, after my father's death, had I made the full distinction between the Royal and the Merchant Navy and it was the latter that interested me for two reasons. The first was that although I liked the Sea Cadets and enjoyed wearing the uniform, I found the authority difficult: 'Left, Right, Left, Right – get in line, Troy,' shouted at me by some bossy kid who, if he'd tried it on in the school playground, might risk a smack in the teeth. I knew one day I'd have to shape up but not yet – Okay?

Peter Joseph Troy

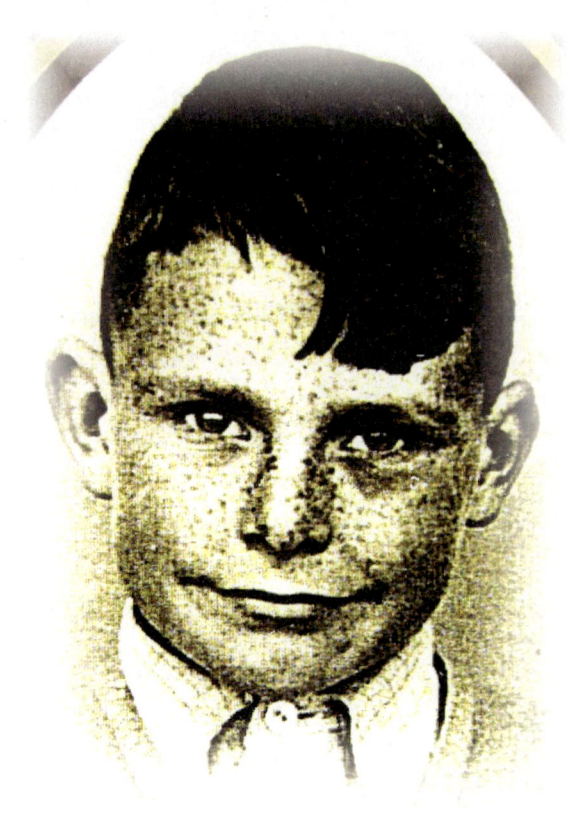

My second reason was Victor's Uncle Snowy, who lodged opposite with them when he was home. When he appeared at the end of our street, on leave with a deep suntan and with his kit-bag on his shoulder I'd get a whiff of the sea and hear the cry of the gulls, which when you thought about it was surprising as we lived nearer Ruislip Lido than the sea. Without removing his kit-bag, Snowy'd get into our game of street footie, giving us a loud radio commentary as he did so:

'*And it's the Hammers all the way, Bond neatly intercepts a pass from Bert Hawkins and head down Bondy's charging up the wing, watch that left foot of his. Brennan attempts a sliding tackle but no, no Bondy's round him and yes, he's still got the ball and yes yes yes he scores with a powerful left... Weh- heh!'*

Snowy wouldn't move on till he'd tackled Kevin Brennan, scored a goal, or put the ball into Mrs Lewis's tulips, in which case we'd all move on a bit smart-like. I wanted to be like Snowy when I grew up, not like Jonesy's dad, who went off every morning to his job selling carpets in Wembley High Street.

Despite all of this it seemed to me, at times, an unrealisable and romantic goal, unlike being a postman, a milkman or a factory-hand, but still it had set me dreaming; like the song said...'*See the Pyramids along the Nile, See the sun rise on a tropic isle....*' I wanted to join up as soon as I was eligible but come on, get real! Could I really see myself steaming across the oceans of the world, perhaps on a tramp steamer bound for Rio or maybe up the Amazon? Were my earlier dreams of seeing the world possible? I knew that time was running out; another year or two and the Army would have me and they'd send me to Colchester like Ernie Blackwell, next door at number 35, and he'd come back dazed, thin and hollow with a short back and sides and dressed in khaki. The Korean War was over but they'd soon find somewhere else to send him to get shot, said Mum.

Like many who had experienced the Blitz, she'd begun to wonder during those post-war years if we really had won the war. 'Our blokes are still fighting and dying,' she'd tell anyone in the queue outside the Co-op, 'and that bloomin' Mr Churchill intends to build a hydrogen bomb,' she'd go. 'He must be off his blinking rocker, cos he must have seen for himself what Doodlebugs and V2 Rockets can do. Yeah so okay Attlee got in, in

1945, and thank God for that, but there's still rationing and long queues, and anything worth having is for export only.'

There were still the long cold winters as well; 1947 had been the worst she could remember and we'd all got into bed together. To keep warm we'd even put what rugs and overcoats we had over the eiderdown. Never a fit man, Dad had wasted himself with booze and tobacco; pleurisy, thrombosis, pneumonia – he seemed determined to collect them all, and his decline accelerated. Mum was fed up with 'Mustn't grumble, dearie' and she'd given up on Vera Lynn with her '*Look for the silver lining*' that was supposed to be behind the darkest cloud when, with the spring in 1948, the sun came out, shone down and lit us all up.

The Council wrote to say that her repeated requests to be re-housed had been granted and we'd all moved into a brand new council house in Belvedere Way, near Kingsbury. She just couldn't believe it – so much space, three bedrooms, our own lavatory and a garden back and front. They were the happiest four years of her life and she'd sing her heart out, polishing the windows, washing the front step and shining the brass knocker. But then the smog of 1952 which fatally curdled itself into people's lungs found my dad's and Mum became a widow.

Mum
(1954)

The Council offered condolences but politely suggested that a family of three no longer required a council house, and would we prefer a cheaper alternative? Where were we to go? The solution was a prefab on the Kingsbury Road, which to be honest wasn't half bad. I was now fourteen and anxious to leave school, so I found work as a van-boy at Restulux, a furniture company in Honey-pot Lane. My job, as assistant to the driver, involved me helping load and unload mattresses and soft furnishings at the factory or at customers' addresses. Then Snodge Oates, who was the upholstery foreman, offered me the chance to learn a trade and began to train me up. But I was still determined to go to sea before the Army got me.

Mum - now nearly forty-four - didn't fully understand why but remaining in the prefab was no longer an option. It dawned on her that she'd made up her mind to move on, even before the Council had. She had experienced the home-front of two world wars in London and wanted something different. No - we were all at a crossroads in our life and big changes lay ahead.

As a widow Mum was now entitled to a pension of five pounds a week but it really didn't go far; if she did take employment then every pound she earned over that amount would be deducted from the pension. Mr Leighton, a publican, offered her part-time employment at The Rose and Crown and although he only paid her seven and six a session it was 'cash in hand' and with the occasional tips it sometimes came to nearly ten bob. As a result she did evening and lunchtime sessions. After Alvar Lidell had finished reading the six o'clock news she'd get ready to catch the bus and go. Rosie and I, as latchkey kids for years, had grown used to her absence and accepted it as the norm.

It was in the pub that Mum first heard of the emigration scheme. Mr Leighton's sister Betty, who helped out behind the bar, had come in one Friday evening full of excited chatter about Canada. 'That's for us,' she'd said. Her hubby, Eric, had applied for details and they'd been sent a large manila envelope stuffed full of information. Coming back on the last bus, Mum's head was full of Betty's chatter: Canada, this and Canada, that! 'Canada!' one of the customers had cried out. 'It's a bloody sight colder there than here.' And with a smile she remembered Sid's comment. 'Bet you can't get Guinness there either,' he'd said as he raised a fresh pint of the frothing stuff to the beaming full moon of his face.

To single men and women

Good Jobs
Good Pay
Good Living

Emigrate to NEW ZEALAND

..for a *NEW* way of life

New Zealand has a place for YOU in her future development. There are many jobs awaiting the new settler.

For **MEN**—Building, Engineering, National Development and Farming.

For **WOMEN**—Nursing, Factory, Domestic and Office.

If you are under 36 **enquire** about the Free and Assisted Passages being offered to **single** British men and women by calling on or writing to the **Chief Migration Officer, New Zealand Government Offices, 415 Strand, London, W.C.2**

Emigration! Another country, the very idea! But it had got Mum thinking. The idea of living somewhere colder didn't appeal but other countries wanted emigrants as well. Australia and New Zealand, on the other side of the world, had day when we had night and their seasons were reversed, which seemed to predict a reversal of fortune.

She sent a letter to New Zealand House for details and when the package arrived she'd opened it straight away. There were a lot of official forms to be filled in and a booklet that gave her the facts about New Zealand. It had a similar climate to Spain and was comprised of two islands. There were photos of beautiful countryside, hills and valleys, beaches and mountains, and the kind of housing that she could expect to find. What's more, New Zealand had been a pioneer of the Welfare State and statistical tables on the cost and standard of living made the country seem ideal. She learnt that as an emigrant she would be expected to stay employed by her sponsor for a minimum of two years, then after that she could seek her own employment. Sponsor? Who would sponsor her? The following day she went up to the New Zealand Government offices in the Strand to find out more about what was to become known as the 'Ten Pounds Pom scheme'.

Sea School

There may well have been a time when previous generations of men and boys had 'run away to sea'. The impression such a term implies is that a man or boy just took off from home, went down to the wharf, found a ship that needed crew and off he'd sail or steam, learning the ropes as he did. In the 1950s it wasn't like that; I didn't just step out of our prefab and go to sea.

The Board of Trade had regulations and anyone wishing to go to sea had to be over sixteen and go through a process which involved a medical and training. The training was designed to toughen a bloke up and was made more demanding than any ship he was likely to serve on. That was the theory anyway. It was thus that on the day following Boxing Day of that same year, 1954, Victor Chivers and I took a train from Paddington to Gloucester. Our destination was The National Sea Training School located on the Bristol Channel at Sharpness. The journey was the end result of enquiries, application forms, a subsequent interview, and then a medical at offices in the East End at Dock Street where a bloke in a white coat felt my balls and asked me to cough.

On the platform at Gloucester station Victor and I found that we were part of a crowd of lads all bound for Sharpness, each with his own personal vision of Victor's Uncle Snowy or my Uncle Jim in mind. Many had arrived earlier by different trains and, as their accents testified, had travelled from a variety of locations. We heard for the first time – not that we understood them – the Brummie, the Scouser and the Geordie.

'Hey you! Jimmy, Jimmy gae us a smoke.' A tough and noisy bloke from Glasgow was busy intimidating and bumming fags off those who were smokers. Officers in naval uniform arrived, bossing us about, and within twenty minutes we were mustered in the station car park and then boarded onto a coach ready to take us to Sharpness. As our coach rolled along the A38 the light of day began to fade, so when we arrived darkness shrouded what was to be our home for the next six weeks.

We were registered, allocated bedding and then marched to a wooden hut in which rows of spindly iron bunk beds stood like vertebrae: angular and vacant in parallel rows. The nippy ones amongst us made a beeline for the bunks nearest the cast-iron stove that stood warm and glowing in the centre of the hut – the only form of heating available. There was a lot of good-natured sarcasm about the luxurious state of the place as we unpacked our gear. 'Gee look, painted breeze blocks, cracked window panes, and wow... even naked light bulbs!' All that was missing was shouts of *'Raus, Raus'*, barbed wire and the barking of German shepherd dogs. Having taken a quick gander at the place some had already done a runner, including the tough Glaswegian with the intimidating manner who had swiftly got back on the coach with enough ciggies to get him north of the border.

As we sorted our gear and made up our bunks one of the blokes produced a rubber hot water bottle and was foolish enough to wonder aloud where he'd get hot water. He immediately became known as 'Hottie Bottle' and remained so for the duration of the course. It was as early as this, within an hour or two of arriving, that I noticed a hard look here and a provocative comment there, as a few of our new intake were already looking to set their reputation as hard-men in the weeks that lay ahead.

I devoured supper that night, something called sea-pie, and what was left over on the plates of some amongst us I quickly wolfed down as well. The journey, the change of air and the falling temperature had given me an appetite that was to stay with me until I left Sharpness. I didn't know it then but that night when I dropped off to sleep, full of hot cocoa and fully clothed in my bunk, listening to the sounds of a harmonica and strange accents, a transformation was taking place. I was seventeen, not yet a man but my boyhood almost a memory.

Although the main part of the camp was nothing more than a collection of wooden huts with corrugated iron roofing, central to the school and what gave it its character was an old sailing ship that was permanently moored on the Gloucester Canal, just off the River Severn. Curiously it was called the *Vindicatrix*: an interesting name, not found in any dictionary but possibly lying somewhere between the verb 'vindicate' (to clear from blame) and the adjective 'vindictive' (revengeful). By deduction therefore it seemed to offer an apology for being spiteful. It certainly explained the situation at Sharpness for the camp was the marine equivalent of borstal: cold showers at 0600 hours, then clad in only vest and shorts, we were marched out onto a dark and freezing parade-ground for a half an hour of physical training. An icy breeze off the Bristol Channel was usually arranged by H.Q. at this time just in case the bromide administered the night before in the cocoa hadn't taken effect; Scouse had spat his out calling it 'anti-wank'. As we stood in columns for a head count someone mumbled something about brass monkeys, but I didn't grasp the significance at the time as having had our balls felt a week or two before, they were now trying to freeze them off.

Whilst I was at Sharpness I was taught to...

1) box the compass

2) tie complicated knots (This one's called a running bow-line. Got it?)

3) learn port from starboard

4) operate a contraption to convert salt-water to freshwater

5) sing 'We are some of the Vindi-boys' and 'Bless-'em-all'

6) call anyone in uniform 'Sir', and lots of other very useful stuff to those of us who hoped to graduate in six weeks as galley or pantry-boys.

Victor and I were billeted in separate huts and had been put into different watches so we didn't see much of each other. Whether he'd taken his boxing gloves down there, because he was never without them, I can't recall but in retrospect I don't think it would have been advisable, or in fact necessary. The camp had several pairs, all obviously well-used, and we new boys were encouraged to try them on. If you didn't volunteer to join the boxing squad then someone did on your behalf, so it wasn't long before we were all paired up to one another for a bout in the ring. Watching and cheering as the sweat and blood flowed, suddenly it was my turn, and I gave a silent salute to Uncle Tom, who had taught me to box in his back yard. Climbing through the ropes and squaring up to a pale, thin, tall and gormless looking bloke from Swindon, who weighed the same as me, I knew I was lucky not to have ended up with one of several tough monkeys who looked the business.

With the adrenalin that fuelled my memory of that moment, I remember so well the bell, the bright lights, the smoky smelly gym and Victor cheering me. 'Go on Joe, knock his block off!'

Encouraged by Vic's words I proceeded to skip forward from my corner, bobbing and weaving with my chin tucked in and letting my eyes glare through my brows. I am by the way a southpaw and was well aware, even then, of the professional and dangerous image I presented. As a cross between Bruce Woodcock and Freddie Mills, I could see I had Swindon petrified of me. He stood centre of the ring, not attempting to defend himself and looking forlorn. I felt the stirrings of pity for him and decided that I'd put him away fairly quickly and not humiliate him any longer than necessary. He was after all some mother's son so I gave him a wink and a nod just to show I held no needle for him – nothing personal – before I demolished him. He must have misinterpreted my look, however. With eyes closed and his face squeezed tight he suddenly rushed forward, long arms flailing from his shoulders. Beset by a desperate panic he windmilled in at me with absolutely no style what-so-ever. Dead easy this one, Troy, I thought, and with my right fist clenched ready for a swift uppercut to put him out for the count I ducked neatly beneath his dread of me. Then the ring juddered as a body hit the canvass. 'It's what's referred to in the boxing world as a "lucky punch",' said Vic, after I had come round. 'Right up until that point though, Joe, it was definitely your fight,' he said as he held my hand whilst the Bosun put two stitches into my lip.

> 'We are some of the Vindi-boys, we are some of the boys.
> We know our manners, we flog our fags for tanners,
> We are respected where'er we go - and as we go
> marching along the street, doors and windows
> open wide – open wide. The Vindi-boys are passing by...'

Vic and I, along with others who had successfully survived the course, sang the words as the coach took us back along the A38 to Gloucester station, all of us glad to be leaving and eager to be away on our first trip to sea. Vic was away to Africa and I was going to Canada.

Before saying a final farewell to the Vindicatrix I would like to pay tribute, along with many others, to ex Vindi-boy Roy Derham MBE, for his determination to reach out and to remind over 70,000 men who trained at the school in their early teens that regardless of where they may be in the world, they are not alone and will always be a 'Vindi-boy'. He founded the Vindicatrix Association in 1993 for the purpose of annual reunions at Sharpness, to rekindle memories and re-establish friendships. The association went global, with reunions currently in Australia and New Zealand. Thank you, Roy!

***

My first ship had been allocated to me at Sharpness during my final week, but after that if I decided not to return for a second trip or wasn't offered a return voyage, then like other seamen I would attend what was known as 'The Pool', a sort of maritime labour exchange, located within the dock area. There were categories or classifications of employment whereby a seaman was either 'established' or not. Never having been an established man I remain unsure of the distinction, although to be 'established' may have offered slightly better conditions of employment, perhaps a better wage or less risk of being flogged or keel-hauled. Whatever it was, to my way of thinking it didn't offer the freedom of being freelance and able to go where I wanted to, and not sent somewhere like Bahrain. They could, if they wanted, send me to the Persian Gulf on a tanker for up to two years with quick turn-rounds and no time in port. Bugger that!

Years later I was to learn that if I had been prepared to become an employee of a company – 'a company man'– then my chances of promotion within the Catering Department would have been greater. The company would offer a career pathway from being a boy rating; say in the galley with training toward being a cook and perhaps a chief cook. If your talents lay in the direction of passenger diplomacy and personnel skills, then maybe you could become Second-Waiter, Head-Waiter or in charge of the bar. Further promotion could lead the individual upward to Second or Chief Steward or maybe even Purser if you had a head for figures and didn't mind learning bookkeeping.

On passenger vessels all of the senior positions within the Catering Department, along with ancillary posts such as stewardesses and ship's writers, who were clerks and manned the Passengers' Information Bureau, were classed as 'Petty Officers' and were collectively known as 'Leading Hands'. They had their own mess-room and better cabins and like the officers they also had the services of stewards and serving staff; quite a cushy number in fact if you were prepared to wear a uniform and were intent on a career at sea. I wasn't that interested in a career whether at sea or not, but just wanted an adventure, a chance to escape post-war London and the stultifying clutch of the early fifties.

Maiden Voyage

There were many occasions on my first trip to sea during which I had cause to remember Big Eric's warnings. Not, I hasten to add, for the reasons he gave. Perhaps if I'd not been so headstrong I might have tried to find out what the reality of it all was like, but then again why would you ever accept another's opinions instead of finding out for yourself?

It was still winter when we left London for St John, New Brunswick, on Canada's eastern seaboard, and the North Atlantic was heavy going. The green and swollen sea caused the vessel to pitch and toss and yaw, ensuring that I threw up any food or drink that I tried to keep down. Dehydrated and with a blinding headache, my limbs and muscles aching from the strain of trying to keep upright, I would stagger each breakfast-time, carrying trays of oily kippers and grilled bacon across the sea-drenched deck from the galley aft to the pantry mid-ships. Between slurps of sweet tea, Frank the pantry-man cautioned me with a tale of a first tripper he'd known who, by continually dry-heaving, had managed to twist the lining of his stomach and had ended his first trip permanently injured and bent double for the rest of his life. Thanks for that, Frank!

After three days I wanted to end it all and wondered if I might be on a charge of 'Absent without Leave' should I throw myself overboard? Getting time off to commit such an act was impossible, however. I was shaken awake every morning at six and by a quarter past was scrubbing a deck that see-sawed so violently that the two buckets beside me – one to scrub from, the other to be sick into – were in constant danger of being overturned and had to be held with a yellow and shaky hand.

After the scrub-out the pantry had to be got ready for breakfast which meant numerous chores to complete: dry stores to collect, boilers and urns to fill and rosies to empty. A pantry rosie contains, until it is full and overflowing, such slops as eggshells, plate-scrapings, tea-leaves and the remains of previous meals. There is a wrong and a right way to empty it at sea, and I was soon to learn that on any vessel there is the weather side and the lee-side, and all rubbish should be emptied over the latter – preferably aft. If I got it wrong and emptied a rosie over the weather-side, for'ard of the bridge, then everything tended to blow back across the vessel, splattering the superstructure and the bridge with tea-leaves, coffee grounds, bacon rinds and the remains of last night's dinner. Depending on the strength of the wind even the occasional empty baked bean tin could find its way up there. They never taught me that at the Vindi.

> Skipper to Mate: 'What the devil's that on the screen number one, soot?'
> Mate (wearily): 'No sir, just tea-leaves.'

During breakfast Frank had me boiling eggs, making toast, ladling porridge and generally fetching and carrying back and forth to the galley whilst two large foamy sinks were steadily filling with greasy pots and pans, eggy plates, cutlery and almost anything else that wasn't battened down in the pantry or saloon. After breakfast, by half past ten, just as I'd managed to get everything washed, dried, put away, and all surfaces swabbed down, it was time to prepare and serve morning coffee.

'Nip up to the bridge with this tray,' said Frank. And while you're at it harpoon any whales you might spot, he could have added, given the absurdity of the situation. The vessel, corkscrewed by a green and angry sea, seemed to conspire with gale force winds in an attempt to dislodge me from an external steel ladder, a ladder to which I desperately clung by one hand whilst with the other I tried to juggle a silver salver on which coffee pots, cream jug, sugar-bowl and crockery were impossibly balanced, the skipper's rich tea biscuits being frisbee'd to the screaming wheeling gulls.

Was it all a monumental wind-up? I asked myself time and again. Apparently not, for neither the skipper nor the mate ever batted an eyelid as I stumbled soaking onto the bridge. More scrub-outs followed; alleyways, heads or mess, then time to begin all over again with lunch at half twelve. The complete cabaret - breakfast, pantry, coffee, scrub-outs - was punctuated with frequent intervals during which I rushed to the side of the vessel (the lee side, always the lee side) where I would lean over and in involuntary spasms spew desperately into the waves.

From the end of the lunch-time strap-up until afternoon tea I had about an hour to myself. Lacking the will to jump overboard I just collapsed into my bunk and fell into an exhausted sleep. Dinner was only a repetition of the previous two meals, same chores, same Frank, same washing-up; only the menu had been changed to protect the cook. Life had become one huge greasy rolling regurgitated meal and I experienced the isolation of seeming to be the only person on board who couldn't share in its doubtful enjoyment. The laughter and rough humour of the crew as they observed my luminous features and Technicolor yawns only set me on a bearing further from them and introduced me to a level of loneliness and misery that hitherto I'd been unaware of. From the depths of my despair a small voice spoke up. Cheer up, it said, things could be worse. So I cheered up and sure enough things got bloody worse.

...and sure enough things got worse

Earlier today, or was it yesterday? I can't be sure for reasons that will become clear. We'd tied up here in St John, and I couldn't wait to get down the gangway. To walk again upon a surface that wasn't continually pitching or rolling had been something I had prayed for, but when I tried to walk the ground seemed to shift beneath my feet and I staggered about. 'Look at him,' shouted one of the deck gang, 'bloody leg-less already.'

There followed much shouting and whistling by several of the crew who, by wicked chance, had followed me down the gangway and onto the freezing wharf.

'I know,' cried the Peggy (the crew mess-man), 'a few drinks should put him right and then he'll walk straight.' This notion then set them off with a lot more wild shouting, and bets filled the air.

'A compensating error,' said a big bald bloke with a ginger beard.

'It stands to reason,' said another who had a ring in his ear.

I wasn't consulted but the Bosun's-mate and the Donkey-man were waving dollar bills about, upping the stakes. The rest, having discussed it, weren't sure but thought it definitely worth a try. My pastoral welfare had become the sole object of our first run ashore and there I was, instantly popular. Everyone – even two greasers from the engine room whom I had never seen before – put their arms across my shoulders and began calling me Joe. Instead of heading for the Seamen's Mission where I'd been intending to go, to post a letter home to Mummy, I found my way with them down-town to a bar called Greasy Pete's. The 'Compensating Error' theory had to be put to the test. Rum with beer chasers turned out to be the very remedy, and the big bald bloke with the beard showed me how to tip them back.

...Amongst a lot of shouting and laughter the Peggy has found some chalk and drawn a line the length of the bar-room floor, then doing an impression of a tight-rope walker he balances and sways wildly along its length. With arms outstretched he encourages others to follow him. But now it's me as I've been selected to be top-of-the-act, and money begins to change hands as bets are laid as to whether or not alcohol is the remedy for one who has finally found his sea-legs the moment he stepped ashore. Giggling, like a loon, I'm being led toward the tight-rope. Someone makes a speech. 'My Lords, Ladeez-an-Genelmen...' Another gives a drum-roll on the bar, and determined to prove for them that alcohol is the answer I proceed to saunter along the chalked tight-rope: 'No prolem, hic, eashy-peashy.' Over-confident and fully into the spirit of it all, I attempt to skip with arms folded in a hornpipe manner...

The hornpipe has been a success and the Peggy is calling for three cheers. Everyone shouts for an encore – but not before another round of drinks. I have never been so popular and happily tip back another rum punch before I oblige to skip another tightrope. Despite hand-on-heart denials someone, however, stretches out a size nine boot and trips me into an adjacent table full of glasses and bottles. An eruption of mirth accompanies my sprawling and wounded body, then much loud argument ensues as bets are called in and more drinks are set up...

...Distant voices are calling me through a fog, and my shoulder is being roughly shaken. Within my bunk a thick pillow of pungent vomit holds my head crusted and secure. I am dead and I stink. It's my stink and it doesn't matter. I can lie there forever and stink forever and nothing matters. The mixture of beer and rum, bought for me by my new found shipmates, had for a while turned the world into a happier place. Surfing now, in and out of what is half memory and nightmare, what's past and what's present has become jumbled. Awareness lurches, then stumbles and intermittently retreats from my brain. Attempting to seek refuge from those who would rouse me I lie inert until they have left to find other amusement. They'll be back though...

Drifting through purgatory I try to recall a time when all had been right in my world and with surprising clarity I see again the day I had joined the ship; it had been the realisation of a dream. The motor vessel *Beaverburn*, owned by The Canadian-Pacific Steamship Company, had been berthed in London's Victoria Docks and I was to join it. Although it was less than a fortnight ago that we'd steamed down the Thames, out into the Channel, around the Lizard and found ourselves on a westerly bearing, it seemed to have taken a month to cross the North Atlantic.

...The pain above my eyes has increased, my throat is parched, and if I move my head I know it will explode, shattering the cabin with snot and gore. I lie still hoping to lose consciousness and retreat again into memory.

The smoke-filled bus from Plaistow, packed with workers, had put me down outside the Dock gates that bitter February morning and hurrying past a line of parked lorries, their tarpaulin covers and ropes sparkling with frost, I'd gone in through the Dock gate, past the duty policeman busy stamping his feet and blowing into gloved hands, and been agog with excitement for

Below Decks

my coming adventure. The canvas kit-bag that Mum made for me sat snugly on my shoulder; it was packed with all the necessities that multitudes of mothers throughout history must have felt were essential for their son's first trip to sea. Amongst my socks and underwear she had packed a Bible, our old alarm clock and a packet of cheese sandwiches. There was also a hundredweight of life's illusions that I'd crammed in when no one had been looking.

1954

Under powerful lights from above, the dock-side even at that early hour was alive with the clatter and clank of industry. My progress was sporadic for I had to stop often to allow great swaying pallets of cargo to be set down or taken up. Forklift trucks, their loads proffered afore them, reversed and spun before me. I passed below the bows of big ships that, straining at their ropes and hawsers, seemed eager to be un-laden and then, with fresh cargoes stored below, on their way to warmer climes.

Out there on the water tugs were mournfully bleating to each other and lighters pushed bow-waves before them. Shunting railway wagons screeched and buffeted back and forth between ships and sheds. Dockers, bundled in scarves and caps, pushed and pulled with hooks at packing cases, pallets and bales. A sharp piney smell of sawn timber perfumed the clear cold air as stevedores, standing high above me on the fo'c'sle of a Baltic trader, shouted to tally-men below, their cockney voices loud and steamy above the racket of clattering winch and running chain.

'Arry, Oi Arry! Bert tell Arry the count's not right, there's only twenny eight, not thirty.'

Arcing through the morning air above my head nets of frozen lamb swung forth but above it all, higher than funnels or masts, the tops of the towering cranes were caught by the first rays of an early sun. Standing splendid and aloof they swung their heavy loads with a majestic ease.

Feeling intensely alive I was filled with a sudden burst of energy. Flicking my kit-bag higher on to my shoulder I saw ahead of me the name *Beaverburn*. As I reached the top of the gangway, the quartermaster on duty reached out a steadying and friendly hand toward me but whoa! Hang about, I thought and remembering earlier warnings about 'friendly' men and Big Eric's 'golden rivet' I declined his help. Okay, so he wasn't at the time wearing a yellow dressing gown but there might have been one in his locker down below. An untidy and restless life had begun to unfold.

...A raging thirst now has me by the throat and loud voices are outside the cabin door. They've come for me again. I stir, wanting to help them and now they're wresting me from my soupy pillow. I'm being lifted bodily and borne away. My head strikes something hard and sharp. 'Steady, steady, careful!' someone cries out as scaffolding collapses within my brain...there's more loud voices... bright lights, blackness and freezing cold beyond a mist. Stripped naked, on hands and knees and on the greasy frozen deck, I'm defenceless as someone laughs. There's a moment, then an oath and a voice shouts, 'Hurry up!' A surge of salty-freezing-sea targets my arse and is hosing me along the deck. It tumbles my body into the scuppers: a violent re-birthing. Splintered, frozen to the core, drenched and retching and with head-splitting giddy awareness I slither and shiver and try to escape.

The hangover, the mother of them all, lasted four days. After which when I did go ashore again I took trouble to go on my own and drank only coffee in Gar's Diner. The home voyage was just as rough but it didn't affect me: I wasn't there but in an 'out of body experience'. Beyond it all I took everything dumbly in my stride and just did the job. My innards, having been turned inside-out, decided enough. Everything actually seemed easier and I began to get on better with the crew. Having experienced what must have been the ultimate in aversion therapy I refused their offered bottles, but they paid me no heed for I had made my bones.

Back at the Victoria Docks in London I signed off the *Beaverburn*. My pay, including overtime, came to eighteen pounds.

'Back next trip?' called the Peggy to me before getting into a taxi with some of the others.

'Wouldn't miss it for the world,' I replied.

Of Bellboys, Wingers and Bloods

Despite my flip comment to the Peggy about not missing a return trip on the *Beaverburn*, I was having second thoughts. The reality of life on a cargo boat as pantry-boy had turned out quite differently from my imaginings of it all. The Merchant Navy was not part of the Armed Forces, but it was considered a reserved and civil occupation: if I stayed in I'd be all right, but if I stayed out too long the Army was sure to get me. I would not be eighteen until the summer so I had a choice and as there was no compulsion to stay on one ship I could shop around for a company to take me where I wanted to go, not where I was sent. Perhaps it wasn't all twelve-hour days filled with drudge and vomit; maybe another company, another ship, some sunshine, maybe a crew of blokes nearer my own age. Yeah! Wow!

The idea was to decide where in the world you wanted to go to, then to find a company whose ships traded there. Fancy the Far East? Try the P & O or the Orient line. Australia, New Zealand? Then nip down to the New Zealand Shipping

Company's offices – but get a haircut first as Baldy Reed in the office is jealous of too much barnet.

'Fancy South America, do you sunshine? Well you want the Royal Mail Line. Ask for Nobby. Tell him Scouse sent you and next time mine's a large one!'

Africa, America, Europe? Just walk into the right office and tell them you're available, show your book and you're away – the world's your oyster! Having had the recommended haircut I presented myself to the catering superintendent, Mister Reed, at the offices of the New Zealand Shipping Company.

'Book?' he asked extending a bony hand, before looking at me. 'We can't have Teddy Boys serving our passengers, can we? Come back when you've had a haircut.'

'But I've just had it done, Sir.'

'Well go and get it done again, get rid of those sideboards or get your money back.'

I went out mumbling under my breath, but I was back within the hour and got the right result. On the 24th of March 1955, I signed ship's articles and was away to sea again, to New Zealand this time as a bellboy on the passenger vessel *Ruahine*. Buttoned to the chin in a close fitting jacket that was cut tight to the waist I looked and felt like Buttons out of Cinderella. I was expected to wear a pillbox hat but having worn it once and suffered comments from almost the entire crew –*'What a cutie'*, *'Hello poppet'*– I successfully managed to lose it.

The *Ruahine* was rated 'Cabin class', somewhere between Tourist and First-class and I had never, apart from the foyer of the Regal Cinema in Wembley, experienced such luxury. The passenger accommodation and dining saloons, lounges and bars were beautifully appointed: walnut panelling inlaid with marquetry displayed fountains, nymphs and doves; sparkling peach-tinted mirrors reflected gleaming brass and chrome. When evening came, the lounges were reminiscent of Hollywood movies where thick carpets and expensive drapes muted the clink of cocktails, laughter and amusing chatter as well-dressed, sophisticated men and women mingled with senior officers, officials of the company and other VIPS.

My part in all this was to be civil, helpful and decorous; or as a waiter later put it, 'We're bleedin' flunkeys.' I didn't mind, I was enjoying myself. It was better than being pantry-boy and besides I was doing all right in tips. That Mrs Williams, for instance, such a stunning mature woman, was more than generous with the occasional florin. 'Thank you, Mrs Williams,' I'd gulp, trying not to stare at her plunging neckline.

It was to be many years before I would seriously question certain assumptions about my station in life, so at the time I could keep playing the game: tug the forelock, adopt obeisance and wear a fixed inane mask. I was seventeen, had respect for my elders regardless and was a product of my time, a prisoner of my youth.

There existed a variety of duties within the Catering Department for boy ratings, and as there were about a dozen of us it was up to the Second Steward as to how and where we were allocated: I might be stood by in passenger accommodation, ready to answer a cabin bell request.

'Sorry, Sir! Baggage room open at ten tomorrow.'

'Yes, Mrs Williams! A large gin and tonic with ice certainly.'

I'd chase back and forth on errands, sound the gong for meals and operate the passenger lift. Mealtimes might find me 'standing-by' in the main dining saloon with Gallagher, another boy rating just starting his first trip. He seemed nervous and had a stammer. Either one of us could be dispatched at a moment's notice to assist a waiter who was 'up the wall', his passengers looking hungry and neglected.

On occasion I might be asked to help out in the children's dining saloon where I would wait at table, assisting mothers to force-feed their children, scrape porridge from the bulkheads and, when the place was empty, scrub the deck and polish the brass. I didn't mind at all any of the duties to which I was put. It was a fun job. Anything was after pantry-boy on a cargo boat.

Our destination was Wellington, New Zealand via the Dutch West Indies, where we'd have about twelve hours at the island of Curaçao, then onto and through the Panama Canal, where perhaps we might have a night ashore in Colon or Balboa. After the canal, the vessel would steam southwest to the New Zealand coast, stopping en-route at the island of Pitcairn for several hours where we'd anchor off to deliver and collect mail.

The outward voyage would take thirty days: ten to reach Curaçao, two to transit the canal and then eighteen to Wellington, crossing the International Dateline just shy of the New Zealand coast at longitude 180 degrees, or thereabouts. It really was up to the 'Old Man'– the skipper, that is – exactly when we were across the date line because at sea he had about the same degree of authority as God. Like the equator, latitude or longitude, the dateline is an imaginary line. It not only separates the western hemisphere from the eastern but also separates two consecutive calendar days. The result is that crossing from the western to the eastern side of the line you lose a day and crossing from the eastern to western side you gain one. On the homeward run from New Zealand, travelling from the eastern hemisphere to the western, the skipper might ordain that we had crossed the dateline on a Saturday and instantly it would be midnight on the previous Friday and Saturday would begin all over again. What he never did was to allow two Sundays back to back because although it might have pleased the vicar, it would mean all crew claiming an extra Sunday at sea, which meant an extra day's paid leave.

On the outward run, however, you could well lose an entire day. Occasionally it was possible to meet an older hand who didn't know exactly how old he was, having completely missed his birthday on a previous trip. There were those of course, who on a homeward trip might have encountered a double birthday, two Saturdays of the same date, which meant that they could celebrate twice. This often led to a double hangover, a certain amount of déjà-vu and theoretically an extra year on one's life.

Not many men can wield that sort of power and it's a factor which should be considered in determining how many skippers run the risk of developing a Messiah complex. Therapists should be aware of this when offering counselling to disturbed ex-sailors who may have made many trips back and forth across the dateline and be totally confused as to their age and when they might reasonably expect to take retirement. Can it lead to premature aging, or an arrested development? There is an enormous amount of material here that never seems to have been explored.

The vessel would spend several weeks on the New Zealand coast, discharging and loading cargo at two or three ports. Then we'd be ready to embark passengers, or 'bloods' as they were known, for the homeward run. The complete, round-trip voyage took over three months, involving a total distance of 24,000 miles.

As the ship approached the Azores the weather began to really warm up and within a day or two the sun began to blaze down from out of a sky that I'd only ever seen in a *'Rupert the Bear'* annual. A holiday-like and more sensuous atmosphere began to pervade the vessel, furthered by the captain's decision to order the rig for the next day to be 'whites'. Gone suddenly were the dark blue uniforms and with them my monkey jacket, thank God. In their place were crisply starched white uniforms, officers and catering crew looking as if we were all involved in an on-going game of cricket or tennis. Taking advantage of the brighter weather the ladies began to dress in a more revealing manner, which of course pleased the males on board and caused me to start examining my own responses to powerful urges that had begun to disturb my sleep and distract my waking hours.

'Oh hello again, Mrs Williams, did you see the Azores? No, I'm off cabin duty permanently; they've put me in the children's dining saloon… Yes it is hot and difficult to sleep… restless and only the single sheet…' (phwoar!)

Even the loose covers and drapes throughout the ship, having realized that high summer had suddenly arrived, transformed themselves into cool pale creams and pastel tints. It was as if the ship and all who sailed in her had passed through a large celestial laundry.

'Don't show him you think it's funny as he'll only do it again,' said Neil's mother in an offhand sort of way as her little boy emptied the contents of his cereal bowl onto the tablecloth and proceeded to slap at it with his spoon and pusher. We were at latitude of about 15 degrees and shortly to arrive in Curaçao, which is best known for the liqueur that was originally produced there. The principal industry since the early part of the 20th century, however, has been the refining of petroleum, a fact that you couldn't fail to register once the ship got within sniffing distance. A pattern had established itself on board and I was working in the children's dining saloon. As I stood by my waiter's dummy polishing a tumbler, and watching Neil construct a small castle from cold porridge, I wondered if there would be any mail for me when we tied up in Caracas bay. During my short leave

Mum had been cracking on with the idea of emigration and I was keen to know how that was going.

Neil was one of ten young children in my care at mealtimes and only one of several, judging by the state of the table, who had plans to become a builder later in life. As soon as he and his mother, who was now getting quite interested and helping surreptitiously with the castle, left the table I could get on with removing the ruins and set up for lunch. I had two tables for five and the brood on my other table had been in and out fairly quickly, I'd changed the cloth and it was now nearly set and ready. The kiddies' saloon was empty apart from my two, and another child with her mum on Spider's table. He'd be in the plate-house having a crafty fag and wouldn't show his face until his last two had gone. In addition to Spider and me there were another two junior waiters, Leo and Steve, four of us to look after forty kids. Leo and Steve had got rid of their little crowd and set their tables ready for lunch, so they'd now be getting stuck into their breakfasts below in the stewards' mess. Neil's mum was beginning to fashion what looked like a turret as I loaded my tray with used crockery and jugs, then ambled out of the kids' dining room, through the main saloon, busy with hungry bloods enjoying their breakfasts, and in through the revolving doors to the Galley.

Once there you were into a different world; the temperature much higher and the noise greater. All was bustle and clatter, orders and steam, as cooks, pantry-men and scullions rushed about with trays and pans, red in the face from their exertions in the heat from the ovens and grills. Waiters, or 'wingers' as they were known, hurried in and out, their demeanour, language and attitude constantly changing, depending whether they were in the Saloon or Galley.

Once he went through the revolving doors and into the heat, gone was the unctuous and smiling Dr Jekyll of a steward that his bloods had come to know and in his place there was a frantic, often scowling Mr Hyde, barking out orders to two or three ancillary stewards who stood behind the hot-press helping to dole out the food.

'Two on the burgoo, three on the Lillian-gish and listen sailor: make it snappy with the toast will ya.'

'She's not up the wall *again*, Sidney, is she?' a calm camp voice amongst the clatter would ask.

'She's always up the wall, this one.'

'Tush, Sidney, she'll hear you and then...'

'Bollocks!' Mr Hyde would bawl back over his shoulder in the general direction of the grinning wind-up merchants, as he balanced his tray, restored his Jekyll smile and disappeared through the revolving doors into a world of civilized calm, potted palms and retired colonels from Cheltenham Spa. No one took offence at this method of communication within the galley – it was par for the course – and besides you'd never get anywhere if you politely waited without giving and taking a load of old banter.

'Mine gone yet?' yelled Spider at me from the plate-house from where he was drying cutlery with one eye half closed against a wisp of acrid smoke from a roll-up wedged into the corner of his gob. I shook my head, 'Nope.'

Peter Joseph Troy

'What in the fuck they doing!' he mumbled sulkily.

'They want more milk,' I said, emptying a full jug of it back into the urn.

'WHAT! You're bleeding joking. Jesus!' He threw cutlery back onto his tray and began buttoning his jacket, the one with the gravy stain, getting ready to go back in and sort them out. I didn't say anything to stop him or give a hint that I was winding him up. He was 'fair game', and besides I didn't like the prat. He'd been in the same job for the past three trips, was one of life's 'know-alls' and not in the least helpful. He was always telling you that which he had least authority to, like how to treat women. *'Let 'em know who's boss, a slap now and again and they'll respect you.'* Or who to vote for...*'Nah, don't ever vote for him, he's a wanker. What you, a class traitor or summing?'*

It was his third trip on the *Ruahine* and he saw us new ones as wet behind the ears. There was something mean about the bloke, and the really annoying thing was that he was always telling you about the things you didn't want to hear from him and never about the things that mattered and would have made the job easier. He'd slyly watch me set my table up completely, saying nothing. Then, just as I was getting my breakfast from the hot-press, he'd say, 'Don't forget it's a silver-dip before lunch.' How he came by the name of Spider I don't know. He did answer to it and seemed proud of it. With a name like that you might imagine he'd scuttle but I only ever saw him swagger. Leo had had enough, and was standing in line to give the creep a right-hander when the time was right.

'Am I going ashore, Mrs Williams? Well yes I am, just for an hour or so as I have to be back to help serve afternoon teas. No,

I'm in the saloon but tea in the cool of your cabin is a lovely idea. Yes I'm sure you can... well I'd like to serve you there but I have to be in the saloon. You could ask your bedroom steward though.'

The ship tied up alongside in Caracas Bay at just about lunchtime, which was fortunate as the bloods, anxious to be ashore, were in and out fairly quickly for their meal, thus allowing the wingers to get ashore quickly too. An advance on our wages wasn't available and only those who were in the know and had money available were flush enough to get a cab into the town of Willemstad, where they'd shop or drink or go wenching. To do so was expensive so better to wait until Panama seemed to be the idea.

Johnnie Murray, a bedroom steward out of Poplar, was making his second trip; knew the score regarding the Kiwi coast and its shortage of decent clobber, and despite the heat was dressed smartly in a powder blue whistle, for he had business in town. With a wedge of readies on his hip he was waiting with other members of the crew under the shade of the deck head for the crew gangway to go down. He'd bought a suit of Wrangler jeans in Willemstad last trip and had worn them frequently enough to make a fashion statement in Wellington and Auckland, thus establishing a seller's market. He'd sold them on for more than double before leaving the coast and this time was going to make a killing, had even borrowed a fiver from Joe Bailey at ten percent to increase his capital.

'Nice bit of schmutter, John,' said the Ipswich Lip, coming up and bogging John's whistle whilst they waited. 'It'll look nice when it's made up.'

'Piss off, Lippy. None of your fifty bob tailor's gear this.'

'No, just joking, John,' goes Lippy, all sincerity now. 'It looks the business, where'd you get it?'

'Bloke I know in Aldgate, does me one every trip,' replied John.

The gangway was nearly down and the small crowd now forming itself into a single loose queue was shuffling forward.

'How much?' said the Lip, nosy like.

'How much d'ya reckon'?

'A score?'

'And the rest.'

'Not a pony? You didn't give a pony?'

Murray should have seen it coming and normally would have done so, but he had things on his mind. It was too late now. They were going down the gangway, the taxi drivers below them beginning to fan out to meet the first of the crowd.

'Must have seen you coming, old son.' Lippy's voice was behind him. There it was -the beginning of the wind up.

'Leave it out, Lippy, you don't get a box back, a finger-tip drape *and* hand-stitched lapels in this material for anything less.' He flung the words back over his shoulder, but he knew Lippy was taking the piss and had done him like a kipper. Still, he'd have him later, and he would too, cos there were never any flies on Murray.

I went ashore about two o'clock with Steve, Leo and Gallagher but as the four of us had to be back to serve afternoon teas we couldn't go far. The heat was scorching as we stepped out from under the shadow of the deck-head and onto the gangway, a heat that I hadn't experienced before. It had been hot since the Azores but the sea breezes had cooled the vessel sufficiently to make it bearable. Now the heat was a hammer. There was a whiff in the sweltering atmosphere; a smell of oily workshops reached us from the huge oil storage tanks that were to be seen within the refinery. Having walked about half a mile along the road from the quay, the blistering asphalt radiating its heat upward and through the soles of our shoes and the sun blazing down upon our unprotected heads, we began to rethink our earlier decision to walk into the town and back. Coming shortly to a Coca-Cola sign outside a dilapidated roadside shack suggested the obvious and we were soon sitting beneath a tattered awning, sharing a drink and listening to each other's jokes and yarns above the chirping of noisy cicadas.

The road had looped around the bay from the quay, so from where we were sat we could gaze back at the vessel, back across a stretch of water that sparkled in the sunshine, and see the ship framed against a blue sky and in literally a different light. From this perspective you could really appreciate her shape and lines, something you just couldn't do when seen midst the grey clutter of the London docks. The first thing that you notice when viewing a ship from a distance is her general shape, her funnel or funnels. Apart from her colours and name that indicate what company she belongs to you might also notice how many decks she has. A passenger ship will have a large superstructure comprising several, and generally they are designated alphabetically. Although the highest deck is usually the boat-deck, thereafter they are A, B, and C as they descend. The captain's cabin and stateroom are usually on the boat-deck or on 'A' deck because they are near to the bridge. The radio officer (known as 'sparks') and senior officers' accommodation is usually on the deck below, which is adjacent to some of the more expensively priced passenger accommodation. On some of these higher decks there are also passenger lounges, bars and venues for leisure activities to take place. Generally speaking, as you descend to the lower decks so the status of crew and passengers descends also. Passengers, therefore, who paid the least for their accommodation used to travel 'steerage', at the lowest level, possibly H deck, just above the bilges where the steering gear for the vessel is located. There was no 'steerage' accommodation on the *Ruahine* or on any passenger vessel sailing out of the UK during the fifties. The practice had ceased some years before.

There existed three main departments on a ship: Deck, Engine and Catering. The Deck department comprised the Skipper, the Mate, deck officers and sometimes cadets, and below them the Bosun, able seamen, ordinary seamen and boy ratings. The Engine department topped down from the Chief Engineer, the Second and then junior engineers and below them there were those employed as donkey men, greasers and - if she was an old coal-burner - stokers. The head of the Catering department on passenger vessels would have been the Purser, followed by the Chief Steward, the Second Steward and leading hands such as the Chief Cook. Then there were galley crew, assistant stewards and boy ratings.

Stewards could be allocated as the tiger to the skipper, which was similar to a batman in the Army or Air Force. There'd be the officers and engineers' stewards, leading hands' stewards, saloon stewards, bedroom stewards, lounge stewards, utility stewards, glory-hole stewards, Uncle Tom Cobbley stewards, and oh yes - boy ratings.

Catering crew had been referred to in the past by a hostile press as 'the lowest of the low'. Whether they acquired such a label because they generally occupy the lowest level of accommodation on any ship or for other darker reasons remains uncertain. Perhaps it goes back to *Treasure Island* when Stevenson made 'Long John Silver' a member of the Catering department.

The cabin that I shared with three other boy ratings was way down, just above the bilges. It was an inboard cabin with a narrow alleyway giving access to a porthole and deadlight. It was small and pokey but what a newcomer might find most inconvenient and claustrophobic was how dimly lit it was.

Coming down from the passenger accommodation, or worse from a sunny deck, was similar to descending into a mine shaft. Each rating had a bunk with a lamp, a curtain for privacy, and also a drawer and a narrow locker in which to keep his belongings. There were four bunks, two up and two down, and it was a hotly debated topic whether it was better to have the top or bottom bunk. It was more convenient to have the lower bunk as you could literally fall into it if need be; but then again so could anyone else (and often did). You had to give consideration also as to who slept above you, for if he was prone to incontinence or sudden vomiting then the advantage wasn't worth having. That's it! Never again, you might decide whilst standing in the shower, having experienced the worst; from now on it's the top bunk for me. Only to discover later, after you had bribed someone to swap with you that the bloke in the bunk below suffered from insomnia and could only drop off to sleep after smoking several pipes of Digger's Black Shag.

Having to live in such conditions caused a certain amount of tension and, despite efforts to be tolerant of one another, as the voyage wore on tempers began to fray and certain people got 'done', Spider eventually acquiring two black eyes on the homeward run. We suspected Leo but he never admitted to it. Had he done so we'd have each bought him a beer.

'You look at his eyelashes and the way he minces about,' said Leo. 'He's definitely bent.' Our conversation and banter beneath the awning of the shack, whilst sipping our cokes, had turned to whether or not the Headwaiter was queer. Poor Gallagher seemed not to have heard of the term. I had begun to think of him as 'poor' Gallagher not only for his stammer and the trouble he had getting his words out, but also because he came from somewhere called D-DDursley.

Steve reckoned it was all to do with wearing tight Y fronts that turned blokes into nine bob notes. I said I thought there was a link with yellow dressing gowns. By now we'd completely lost Gallagher, but then – with respect – he had grown up on a pig farm.

'Mind you,' said Leo. 'I've got nothing against them, cos look at it this way, they're doing us all a favour if it means more crumpet for us.'

Our cokes were finished and so was the tutorial. Time was getting on so we stepped out from under the awning into the bright heat of day again.

'See, Gallagher, what you gotta understand is there really are blokes who want to be women. They like women and women like them but they just can't get it up see.' Steve was attempting to explain to Gallagher all about queers as we made our way back to the vessel. Stopping briefly, we looked at the remains of an old fort said to have been erected by Henry Morgan, the Welsh buccaneer who sacked Panama City during the seventeenth century and after being knighted eventually became Governor of Jamaica.

There was a blue aerogramme letter for me that I found on my bunk when I got back. It was from Mum telling me that by the time that I received it she and Rosie would no longer be living in the prefab but would have moved in with her brother

Dick and his family in Battersea. Things had happened quite quickly since I left, but that was just like Mum: she didn't hang about. Her letter went on to tell me that she had gone up to New Zealand House and talked to someone about sponsorship, which had saved a lot of time and bureaucracy. A certain Mr Coleman needed a housekeeper on his sheep station near a place called Masterton in the North Island and she'd sent him a letter, explaining her situation. Furthermore Uncle Dick had generously offered me lodgings whenever I was on leave. The problem of accommodation when I was back in London hadn't really occurred to me. It just wasn't an issue, a fact I suppose which indicated my state of mind at the time. I must have felt that the world was a very benign place in which to be and there would always be somewhere to stow my gear or a bed in which to sleep.

'More tea, Mrs Williams?' She had decided after all to take tea in the saloon as it was cooler than in her cabin...

The ship left Curaçao after dinner that evening and as our duties delayed us until after shore leave had expired we were unable to get ashore again. But there'd be time to explore when we stopped here again on the homeward run.

The Panama Canal

Panama exports petroleum products, bananas, shrimps, copper, hangovers and the clap. The canal is about fifty miles in length and crosses the Panama Isthmus; it was started in 1879 by the French engineer De Lesseps but left unfinished when he died. Taken over by the American government in 1904, the project took ten years to complete, and such is the difficulty of the terrain that the canal requires twelve locks. This fact, plus the chance to observe alligators, snakes and other wildlife, adds to the interest of making the transit. Another, less well known, statistic is that for every yard of progress in excavating the canal a life was reputed to have been lost from swamp fever and accidents.

There was an advance payment on our wages the day before we arrived at the canal, and everyone was taking advantage of it, or so the length of the queue waiting outside the leading-hands mess seemed to indicate. I took a fiver and exchanged it for American dollars. It was about ten days' pay at the time so I felt flush and extravagant in doing so. The ship was going to transit the canal before staying overnight in Balboa, which seemed to excite many of the crew. Balboa is the port of Panama City and was preferred by those who knew the Canal Zone and could compare it to Colon, the port at this, the Atlantic-Caribbean end of the canal. There was much reference made by those who were in the know to somewhere called The Teen-age Club and Spider looked knowing and adopted his man-of-the-world mantle. 'You blokes'll be okay if you stick together; best get someone to take you ashore but don't ask me, cos I've got a bird here and I won't want you lot following me about.' The lads had got his number so didn't even give him the benefit of their curiosity, preferring to satisfy it by asking questions of others instead.

Standing under a cooling shower in the stewards' ablutions was a pleasant experience and I was in no hurry. Dinner for the bloods had been early and the vessel was due to dock at Balboa in about an hour's time, at ten o'clock. I was going ashore with several others, going 'mob-handed' was the expression. The ablutions-room was large with plenty of facilities and at the time was busy with towel-clad stewards coming and going, all getting ready for a full night ashore, the first since leaving London, nearly two weeks ago. Other showers were available and no one was waiting so I was lazily enjoying the tepid water, washing away what remained of thoughts about Mrs Williams, plus the heat and rush of what had been a long and sticky day. Out from one of the showers, with a towel about him, and drying his hair vigorously stepped a pale and pimply body. It was Spider. He approached a nearby basin and fumbled in his toilet bag bringing forth a small tub of Brylcreem. It was rumoured that in his locker he kept a large carton of the stuff. Having dried his hair he began to drag his comb through it, occasionally holding the comb under the running tap. Holding up the Brylcreem to the light he checked its quantity, removed the lid and gently topped it up with water from the tap. Replacing the lid he briskly shook it up and down like a cocktail, then taking up a central position in front of the mirror above the basin and with legs slightly bent he unscrewed the lid from the tub and empted its contents directly on to the top of his head. Quite why I was so totally absorbed in his actions remains a mystery to me but for some reason I was. Maybe Spider's absorption in his personal grooming was contagious. So totally absorbed were we both that we didn't even notice if others were too. With great care he massaged the globby white blob into every part of his scalp, and then proceeded to comb his hair slowly and methodically into its Tony Curtis style, occasionally flicking the residue of grease and water off his overloaded comb into the basin.

Turning his head first this way and then that, Spider assessed the creation from the side of each eye in turn – first port then starboard and steady as we go. He combed the sides upwards at the front into a roll on the top that was then coaxed forward to cascade down over his brow. The remainder was combed backwards terminating in what was supposed to resemble a duck's arse and known as a D.A. When he'd finished his head gleamed with not a hair out of place. The completed masterpiece resembled a large crow-black meringue that had been varnished and lacquered onto his head. Fumbling once again into his toilet bag Spider produced shaving gear but the show was over for me, the spell broken. Time was getting on but the cabaret had been strangely satisfying.

'*Nosostros vamos, quanta costa?*' asked Kelly loudly, enunciating his fluent Spanish. He was the scullion and it might have been his Belfast accent for the Spanish cabbie couldn't seem to understand so said nothing. We were on the dock arranging transport to the city. Kelly went into an exaggerated mime of driving a car, his large fists turning back and forth an imaginary wheel. Then pointing to each of our little mob in turn, and including himself, he counted loudly.

'*Uno, dos, tres, quatro*, er– five,' he added, holding up five pudgy fingers before repeating the magic words, '*Nosostros vamos, quanta costa*? Five dollars yeah, okay?' The cabbie still said nothing but shrugging his shoulders, opened the rear door to the Mercedes taxi and beckoned three of us into the back. Kelly, looking pleased with himself, squeezed into the front beside Leo who had already entered the cab before the pantomime had finished.

'Where to?' said the cabbie, switching on the ignition.

'Anywhere downtown,' replied Kelly.

The humidity was high and my drip-dry shirt was already soaking as we piled out of the cab somewhere central in Panama City. There occurred some delay whilst Kelly, his T-shirt riding halfway up his back and displaying the hairy cleavage of his buttocks, bent forward to pay off the cabbie. With his large head and shoulders wedged through the open cab window we could hear him arguing in a loud voice with the driver about the fare. 'We agreed five bucks and no more,' he shouted. It was sorted eventually and the cabbie took off, gunning the engine, burning rubber and looking angry. 'Bleedin' dago-wops,' went Kelly as he gave the departing cab two fingers.

Neon lights flashed their rhythmic message on and off and on again whilst blaring music pumped its Cuban rhythms and heady brass from bars into the sultry night. There seemed to be a menacing promise in the fetid air as we wove our way along the crowded sidewalk. Advancing slowly through the colourful crowd we were jostled by men and women young and old, children carrying babies and baskets, some peddling fruit, vegetables and jars filled with... well maybe it was liquor, I could only guess. Shopkeepers beckoned. 'Senors, ello. You Inglish?' they asked, their mustachio'd grins attempting to interest us in trinkets or clothing.

I must have loitered whilst drinking in the sights for suddenly I realized I'd lost sight of the others. Steve had been just in front of me, behind Leo. Now neither was to be seen. The other two, Kelly and his mate –whose name I'd forgotten but who had been with Kelly on the *Dominion Monarch*– had taken the lead but they were nowhere to be seen either. A moment of panic as a man, his face like aged leather with teeth to match, tugged at my sleeve and tried to sell me a watch. Nervously I brushed him away, peering anxiously about to see if I could recognize Leo's tall figure, with crew-cut and in a blue T-shirt. Where were they? Perhaps I'd overtaken them and they were all back there behind me somewhere. Should I go back or maybe wait? Better to press on.

Hurrying along I suddenly spotted the burly shape of Kelly down a narrow side street and immediately saw Leo and the others about him. They seemed to be handing him money. I allowed myself a breath of relief, relaxed and slowed my pace, trying to appear totally cool as I approached them. I had the edge as they hadn't seen me, perhaps hadn't even missed me. A tall Negro was talking and pointing through an open door, over which flickered a broken neon sign, and had their attention.

Halting beside them I said to Steve in my Bugs Bunny voice, 'What's-up-doc?'

'Where've you been?' Steve replied but then without waiting for an answer said, 'We're going in.' We all trooped in behind Kelly, the Negro pulling chairs out from a large round table and waving over a waitress.

'Rum and coke's the drink in this place,' Kelly told us and we - men of the world that we were - nodded. He ordered for us all from the waitress who was young, black and smiling broadly. We were seated in the corner of a large, high-ceilinged barn of a place, the air reeking with the stale aromatic yesterdays of Cuban cigars and brilliantine. Tables and chairs were ranged against three walls, the fourth wall taken up by the bar, which ran its length and at which several ladies of the house sat on high stools. There were no windows but two or three wall-mounted fans stirred the humid air about and provided an intermittent breeze. A large central raised platform was obviously the dance-floor and stood between where we were seated and the bar, but the place was practically empty. A wide stairwell descended from what appeared to be a minstrel's gallery and led directly onto the dance floor. You could therefore dance straight up the stairs if you felt particularly inclined to do so. What you did with your partner after that was almost anyone's guess.

The place had a feel of an old wild-west bar-room or frontier casino about it and should Joel McCrea have appeared on the gallery above, perhaps slugging it out with a cowpoke or two, then no one would have been too surprised. Either that or I had sat in front of too many cowboy movies on Saturday mornings.

'A crowd of us were in here last trip,' said Kelly's mate. 'We had a great night,' he added as our smiling waitress put down before us five tall tumblers of crushed ice with a fat finger of rum in each and five frosty bottles of coke.

'We're a bit early but it really livens up about midnight,' he added, shelling out dollar bills and grandly waving the change away.

'Well it needs to,' said Leo as he made a grab for a bottle of the iced coke. 'There isn't even any music.' He rolled the frozen bottle of coke under his chin and across his throat then let out an ecstatic sigh.

'Music! Leave it to me,' said Kelly, 'I'm going for a leak, then I'll arrange it.'

'Ask if they've got any jazz while you're at it,' said his mate.

As it was only about ten o'clock I made a mental note to take it easy on the rum and coke because if you were worried about your response to it, like I was, you could really drown it with ice and coke and thereby control your level of intoxication and subsequent hangover. Well, that was my theory anyway.

'It's all arranged,' said Kelly, back from the bog and as he spoke someone behind the bar started messing about with a tape recorder.

'See,' he added. After two or three false starts the strategically-placed speakers crackled into life and Peggy Lee's sexy tones began to give us 'Fever'.

'This ain't jazz,' complained Kelly's mate. 'Patience, old son, patience,' said Kelly.

Halfway through 'Fever' someone really wound the volume right up and at this point, as if on cue, there was definitely an increase in the interest level by the ladies at the bar. It was like tea break was over and 'back to work, girls'. They swung their stools around and, with increasingly bold looks in our direction, began giggling more openly and whispering to each other. Two of them got up on the platform and began to dance together, their bodies swaying provocatively.

...The bottles and glasses on the wet tabletop would indicate that we are now into our third or is it the fourth round? Who cares? Who's counting? Kelly's mate is into another joke concerning an Englishman, an Irishman and a Scotsman but Kelly must have heard it before as he seems more interested in the dusky girl who's straddled across his knees facing him, her short skirt hiked high on her thighs. To be honest I too find her more interesting than the joke and fail to get the punch line when the joke is over, but I laugh along with the others anyway.

Suddenly there's a lot of whooping and clapping as a crew of Yankee sailors, who had entered shortly after us, are encouraging one of their own into an Astaire-like tap dance on the table-top. Others in the bar share in the cheers too, and good humour is high. There are about twelve yanks and they're friendly. One of them calls over to our little mob and toasts us with his glass. We reciprocate with grins and Leo begins to hum 'Anchors Away', which pleases them. I experience a feeling of camaraderie for all Americans as it was these guys who not only got us through the war but also brought a type of music over and entertained me through my childhood with the bright American comics that found their way into the damp playground of Elms Lane School.

One of the sailors, a tall skinny fellow with a bobbing Adam's-apple and his hat clenched to his chest sings 'Maybe it's because I'm a Londoner' in an imitation cockney voice. Kelly doesn't look too amused, but I suddenly realize I'm having the best time of my life. 'Give us a fag,' I say to Steve before I remember I don't smoke. The floor before us is filled with swaying and smooching couples. Leo is up now, looking a bit self-conscious, but dancing well with a tall slender mulatto girl, her body welded to his, hips gyrating. It's a Lena Horne number, the singer's tantalising voice oozing the words through crackly speakers and into the smoky atmosphere, rousing something primeval and urgent within me.

'...It's just an old fashioned tango - and there's
nothing to it. You just sort of stand there and
just sort of do it... The floor may be crowded but...'

The place is beginning to get crowded and smoky and I recognize more faces from the ship. The 'Ipswich Lip' and two of the galley crew are propping up the bar. We catch sight of them, shout into the babble and give them the thumb. The Lip points at Leo, still dancing, slapping his right palm suggestively several times into the crook of his left elbow. Kelly, now with an empty lap – the girl gone – laughs and returns the action. Another tray of drinks arrive and so far I haven't paid for a thing, not even the cab. Better sort it out now, I think and reach for my roll of bills but Steve stops my arm and points at Kelly, saying something above the music, noise and babble which I fail to understand.

It's time for a pee, so I rise and thread my way through the throng of dancers on the platform toward a door with a picture of a Disney Caballero on it. A Yankee sailor comes out and holds the door for me: 'Okay, feller!' I nod and go in. The place is dimly lit and stinks of stale smoke, piss and Old Spice shaving lotion. I hold my breath as I stand at the urinal, which is nothing but the wall with a gutter below it, and while I empty my bladder I take a private moment to assess my condition. I'm okay, a bit high but definitely not over the top, and because I don't want another bloody hangover, I resolve to stay that way. When I get back to the table we've got company. The tall mulatto girl is straddling and jigging across Leo's knee. Two more are hovering attendance and a plump one, more woman than girl, is sprawling, legs apart, in my seat, an American sailor's hat perched on the back of her head amongst a mass of luxuriant curls. It's her unbuttoned blouse that teasingly reveals most of her full breasts that rivets my attention.

Apart from gaping, I'm not sure what to do and feel a bit awkward so turn away, but the woman solves my indecision by reaching out a plump brown arm and pulling me backwards onto her lap. Putting both arms about my waist she laughs and nuzzles the nape of my neck. Nothing like this has ever happened to me before – well okay, Aunt Monica did once, but that was different. This one now begins to rock me on her lap and sticks her tongue in my ear. I get an instant... well reaction. WOW! I look at Steve, not really wanting to be rescued but perhaps maybe for a clue, but Steve's occupied also. I can't see his face as it's curtained by a mass of dark hair, the owner of which seems to be busy leaning over whispering or kissing his ear. Kelly catches my eye and, gives me the hand/elbow sign, grinning lewdly.

Her hands have found their way inside my shirt and she's pinching and stroking my nipples. I ought to tell her to stop but I don't want her to – ever. 'You give me cigarette, yes?' she whispers into my ear, her warm breath and wandering hands making me feel all heavy in my saloon blues. Taking a liberty I lean forward and nick one of Steve's Woodbines without bothering him. He seems fairly busy and might not welcome the intrusion. I turn to pass her the cigarette over my shoulder and I'm looking into warm brown eyes, and not wanting her to stop what she's doing with her hands. She takes the ciggy between her lips, her eyes holding mine, then she whispers again, her hands (ooh!) slipping their way downward, becoming bolder.

'Such a big boy! You like to be a naughty boy? You come upstairs with me, yes?' Nothing quite like this happened behind the bike sheds at Claremont Secondary Modern so I'm sort of scared - but yes! I'm melting away inside and want nothing more than to go upstairs with this woman and be down and dirty. Yes. Oh yes please! She fondles my need and knows exactly what I want, what I'm craving for.

'You cherry-boy I can tell. I make it nice and slow for you, yes? Me very good with young lovely boy like you. Only ten dollars.' She puts the tip of her red pointy tongue into my ear again, making a low moaning sound, and my Y fronts tighten like a noose.

Steve takes this highly charged moment to tap my arm, bringing me reluctantly out of my erotic trance. Grinning he beckons me in with his head, he wants a word, and I give him my ear, still moist. In a quiet voice Steve asks how I'm fixed for money. Can I lend him four bucks as he's a bit short and something's come up? If he's feeling anything like me, I've got a fair idea exactly what it is that's come up but I don't start any smart dialogue; I like Steve and reach for my wad, still complete with an elastic band about it, and peel him off four green singles. Steve winks, and his dusky girl pouts me a kiss and says something in Spanish to my woman before leading Steve off in the direction of the stairway.

Before I can get back to the business in hand, and I'm eager to believe me, I'm aware that Kelly and his mate are preparing to leave.

'We're off to The Teenage Club. You wanna come?' he asks. 'We've got a cab; it's only about 20 minutes.' I look around for Leo but he isn't at the table or on the dance floor. He's probably gone upstairs as well, as the tall mulatto isn't to be seen either. I don't want to leave at that moment; I really don't and so decline, saying that I might go over later with the others. My woman gives me a squeeze, supporting my decision and reminding me of the mystery that lies just up the stairs.

'Okay!' nods Kelly. 'You'd better fix up what you owe now. What's it come to, Kevin?'

'Twelve bucks and that includes the fare for the cab here,' replies Kelly's mate, who it now transpires is called Kevin.

'Tell the others they each owe the kitty another two, but we'll see them later,' says Kelly absently.

Twelve dollars! That much, I think, taking out my roll and peeling off two fives and two singles. I pass it over to Kelly, who passes it to Kevin. Twelve, plus four to Steve, I'm doing the arithmetic and that comes to sixteen which only leaves me about eight dollars and out of that there's a cab to pay to get back to the ship.

***

I remained celibate and almost sober that night. I kept my cherry but it wasn't by an act of will or for any moral consideration: I just couldn't raise the necessary ten dollars to discover the mystery that lay up those stairs and that had been vaguely beckoning me since the onset of puberty. Intense frustration and disappointment flooded through me when I realized that I wasn't going to be able to experience the delights that an exciting woman had been promising for just ten dollars. That elemental part of my nature that had been bothering me since way back and had grown in strength since the Azores, that vital and essential ingredient which one day was to ensure the continuation of my genes, had been primed by that woman in that place. Its blue touch-paper had been lit, my rocket set and ready for take-off to the stars.

For many weeks after I replayed fantasies night after night. Reels of pornography whirred in the dark intimacy of my bunk as the five-fingered widow held me in her grip of lust. My fantasies became almost tangible: always with that woman, and only that woman, in that place and up those stairs. It left me for years with an interest in older women and an urge to get back to Balboa.

Before the ship got as far as the Galapagos Islands a day or two later, any remaining hangovers from the night ashore had been dispelled by the clean warm breezes of the Pacific Ocean.

We had, however, picked up a stowaway. In fact more than one had made themselves known within a day or two. They were microscopic and had been hiding in various urethras and were known colloquially as a dose or the clap. Poor Spider! Ha-ha! After a visit to see the ship's doctor he was relieved of his position in the children's saloon and put to utility duties: scrubbing decks, polishing brass and cleaning the heads. Despite my initial disappointment I now felt immensely relieved that I had 'behaved' myself and began to follow the example of many of the others who, hypocrites that we were, when anywhere near Spider would ring an imaginary hand bell and shout 'unclean, unclean'.

Speculation and debate on gonorrhoea and other diseases that were venereal in nature became rife in the Stewards' mess. Long discussions ensued about the legendary 'umbrella treatment', the prospect of which made us wince. It would inhabit many a man's room 101, and something similar might become a reality later in life for any man prone to prostate problems. Leo and Steve, being what you might call 'interested parties', were often to be found present at such discussions and at times began to look quite worried.

'Well at least Spider knows it's only a touch of the guns and not syphilis,' said Tiny, one of the cooks, addressing the mess generally one night during dinner. He stood much taller than the dartboard into which he was habitually flinging darts and was a source of irritation to many whilst we ate. Given the sour disposition and raw aggression of the bloke, however, who was going to tell him to stop?

'Why's that then?' ventured Leo, a bit too interested. Tiny didn't respond for a moment, he was taking careful aim, the concentration squinting his eyes and protruding the tip of his tongue between fat wet lips. He was going for double twenty at the top of the board.

'Because... sod it! Because...' He paused for effect. '...If it was syphilis he wouldn't know he had it until his nudger fell off.' He strode to the board to collect his darts, one of which had fallen. An obligatory and sycophantic laugh went around and then Reg, one of the wingers sitting at a table with his feet up and rolling a fag, spoke. 'S'right!' he exclaimed. 'S'dead-right.' He endorsed Tiny's opinion before adding '...and when he bent down to pick up his nudger, his eye-balls-ed drop out. S'right init, Tiny?'

Tiny didn't answer, or even grin. He didn't have to. He didn't need anyone's endorsement: no one was going to share his joke or steal his thunder. He gave Reg a nasty look; he had a certain status to uphold. He was a hard-man and one way of reminding you of the fact was to speak only when he wanted to. He didn't have to answer questions or agree with anyone, certainly not the likes of Reg anyway.

Peter Joseph Troy

To the Land of the Long White Cloud

As the ship steamed further into the Pacific Ocean a relaxed routine began to develop on board. It had been over two weeks since the *Ruahine* had left London and by this time each member of the crew was well acquainted with what was required of him and performed his tasks for the day like a robot. Faces and personalities were no longer strange but had been acknowledged. Yes mate, no mate, okay mate had been replaced by yes Fred, no Mike, okay Doug. Each idiosyncrasy if not accepted was at least tolerated. Shyness, that affliction that no seaman ever admits to but is none the less quite common, had been banished by a patina of familiarity.

The day dawned surprisingly cool each morning considering the humidity experienced during the night by those who had lain uncovered and restless on their bunks in the sticky cabins below. The sun as it peaked above the eastern horizon suddenly flooded the vessel with a peachy pink radiance that lent splendour to the most mundane of chores, even the early morning beer-carry. Bleary-eyed stewards, their faces puffy with sleep, turned to at six-thirty and plodded their way to the storeroom for that - their first chore of the day. Two cases, or a keg, per man had to be carried along alleyways and up several companionways to the bars that were on the higher decks. Not quite the hair of the dog, but at least a livener to the day. After the beer-carry there followed the mandatory scrub-out; buckets, brushes and Brasso were handed out from the glory-hole by a utility steward, so each man could sweep and scrub a section of deck, and maybe polish the brass-work for which he was responsible. When that was finished there might be time for a quick cup of tea before a shower and getting dressed, ready to serve breakfast.

Up on deck in that early morning light with a cup of tea beside me on the hatch was a time for brief reflection, and I often found myself thinking about friends and family back home. It took a little mental adjustment to compute what time it might be back in the cold UK. Were they asleep back there or maybe just getting ready for bed? The days seemed to flow effortlessly into each other. During periods of leisure between duties most members of the catering crew were to be found up on deck, working away at their suntans whilst they dozed or read or twanged a guitar. The next port of call was Pitcairn Island where we were to anchor off for several hours, whilst mail and perhaps medical supplies were delivered. On arrival there would be no shore leave or trips for passengers although sometimes the Doctor went ashore to minister to whoever might need it. Many of the Islanders rowed out and clambered up rope ladders to swap souvenirs and sell fruit to all on board. The souvenirs comprised wooden carvings or woven goods. I swapped a shirt and a pair of plimsolls for a wooden flying fish but wondered who the plimsolls were for. They certainly weren't for the man with whom I traded, for his bare feet, like most of the Islanders, were enormous: the largest that I had ever seen.

The Islanders were of course descended from the mutineers off H.M.S *Bounty* and their Tahitian womenfolk, who had populated the Island in 1790. In 1955 the total population was alleged to be about fifty. So much has been written about the mutiny and its main characters, Bligh and Christian, that there remains very little new to say about the affair. But as an aside I might mention that some years later - in 1961 - I was in Tahiti for several days on a much smaller vessel, the *John Wilson*, working my passage out to New Zealand, and we were berthed behind a replica of H.M.S. *Bounty* on which filming for a new version of 'The Mutiny' was taking place. A few of us were invited on board when filming had finished as celebrations were in progress for one of the film crew who had married a Tahitian woman. We never saw Brando or Trevor Howard but shook hands with Richard Harris, Noel Purcell and others of the cast. The replica *Bounty* was an amazing vessel with air-conditioning and even a coke machine installed below. The wreck of the original, which had been burnt, lay on the sea bed just offshore.

From the Panama to Wellington, apart from the brief stop at Pitcairn, each day was a transparent overlay of the preceding and following days with very little to distinguish between them. A general lassitude and boredom was developing amongst the crew and amongst many of the passengers too. Eighteen days at sea seemed a long time and way back then there was of course no satellite television or radio. The only music available below decks in the crew accommodation was that played by a crew member who may have brought his old wind-up record player along with him, plus a heavy stack of 12-inch records. There was occasionally a guitar or maybe a harmonica but if you weren't into country and western sung by the baker's boy then you had to wait till you got ashore to listen to Elvis, jazz or rock-n-roll. As a result there existed a lot of free time between duties, which, if you didn't read, was given over to scuttlebutt, rumours and yarning, usually in the stewards' mess.

Alcohol was not freely available to the crew, although those who had adult rating were issued two small bottles of lager or beer daily from the store, which were signed for, put on a man's tab and taken out of his wages. Some of the crew would draw their allocation, then store it or sell it on to those who really liked a drink. On some ships, I was later to learn, and dependent on the level of desperation of those who enjoyed getting out of their heads, there were alternatives to a bottle of lager. There was a way of extracting the alcohol from Brasso or Old Spice shaving lotion. What you did was to nick a stale loaf from the bakery, you cut off each end of the loaf and using it as a filter you set up your own still. The brewing time could be anything from forty-five minutes to overnight. This process was sometimes carried out on tramp steamers and tankers, which could be away from the UK for anything up to two years, and the results could lead to momentary bliss, hangovers, arguments, mutiny, murder, mutilation and rape on board certain vessels: one of the reasons why the skipper on any ship was permitted to possess a firearm.

It was this sort of information, often relayed by – and to – those who had gathered for a bit of a yarn over a late night cocoa in the mess, that kept crew members up until past midnight and led to bleary eyes at dawn. The ability to relate a yarn or a joke and usually by a man who had 'been about a bit' and was therefore into his forties or fifties was more than enough to award status to the individual and assure a degree of deference and respect to him. Some of the older guys had been at sea during the war, but seldom did they talk about the horrors that they might have experienced. They, however, were always guaranteed an eager audience of younger listeners.

Eighteen days were proving to be difficult for the bloods as well, despite the varied social program laid on: dances, fancy dress evenings, horseracing events (with a board and dice), even the occasional film. About once a week, after dinner, a large screen was erected on the rear well deck and a film projected for all to watch. It was always popular and attracted those of the crew who were not on duty. We would watch sitting or lolling on a lower deck or the hatch-cover whilst the bloods sat comfortably on the deck above.

It was during this time, two weeks after leaving Panama and within four to five days of arriving on the New Zealand coast that the master-at-arms and the watchmen became more vigilant as irritations amongst the crew boiled over into loud arguments that often became fistfights. Men, following tradition, solved their problems between themselves and anyone who grassed to an officer became reviled at the very least, and on some vessels he might even disappear. Risks were taken as illicit assignations were arranged between passengers and crew, with often-dire consequences. It was forbidden for any member of crew, apart from the officers, to meet and socialise with the passengers. If a crew member was caught then he risked at least a logging (his conduct would be entered into the captain's log for the voyage) and he'd lose a day's pay. At worse he might get a D.R. (decline to report) in his discharge book at the end of the voyage; a 'D.R' stamped in red was serious enough to ensure that he would have difficulty in finding employment on any vessel that was halfway decent. Female passengers, especially those travelling alone, were sometimes fascinated by the crew members with whom they came into contact, particularly the stewards and even more so the bedroom stewards. A dashing figure with charm and charisma presenting the wine or offering cabin service with a twinkle in his eye was enough to set a young and impressionable heart – thousands of miles from promises and responsibilities – all of a flutter. Warm Pacific nights with a smooth swell on a following phosphorescent sea, the lull of the gently rolling vessel, the Southern Cross, the moon and stars so bright, so clear... 'It was like taking candy from a baby,' said Morton, one of the wingers, who came from Bootle but looked like Errol Flynn. It wasn't until the homeward trip weeks later that he spilt the beans about what he and Mrs Williams got up to the night the rest of us were ashore in Panama. After that they'd been at it on a regular basis across the Pacific. It was only then I realized with hindsight, doom and gloom it could have been me.

There didn't at that time exist a charge of intercourse, sexual or otherwise, with the passengers because in the early days of trading anything being transported on board was considered cargo, and maritime law had never been updated to include passengers. If a crew member was found in a 'compromising position', or to dispense with the euphemism, if he and a female passenger were caught vigorously shagging each other, both completely naked in her bunk, then not only was it 'coitus-interruptus', but conclusions might be jumped to and although reasonable explanations might be thought up and offered, he could find himself on a charge of 'Broaching the Cargo'.

***

'When they come in, be ready to pull out the chairs for the ladies.' The captain's tiger seemed nervous as he explained the procedure to me. It was nearly seven-thirty and I had been seconded by the headwaiter to help him serve dinner on the captain's table. Although it would be at least another thirty-six hours before we arrived in Wellington it was the Farewell Dinner and something of a special occasion with a special menu. Those passengers who had been honoured to dine with the captain throughout the trip were treated as VIPs. The reasons for such distinction were varied; they may be senior officials of the company and their wives, they may be celebrities or they may have a title. The total in number was only eight so I couldn't understand the tiger's nervousness. It should be a doddle: two of us to serve a civilised eight! I wondered how he would have coped with my brood in the kid's saloon: ten of them, some in high-chairs, and at one time or another usually yelling, spitting or hurling their custard and jelly at one another.

In retrospect though, I was to understand the tiger's nervousness and glad to get back to the dippy egg and jelly brigade. As his *commis* I would merely be assisting him and not really serving at table; that was his job. My job was to fetch and carry to and from the galley and generally make myself useful.

The dinner gong was about to be sounded and passengers were waiting just outside in the foyer to enter the saloon and take their seats. The wingers in freshly laundered and starched white jackets were standing to, waiting for the off, a little light banter going on, a chuckle here or there usually at the expense of those waiting to come in.

'Here they come, any moment now, like a load of bleedin' vultures!'

'Mick! Oi, Mickey! If she's showing out up front again tonight, I dare you drop a sprout down there.'

The Farewell Dinner was often 'dropsy-night' for the lads, a little 'thank you, steward, for all your attention throughout the trip', and envelopes were discreetly passed into expectant palms. The gong – a small hand-held xylophone - was sounded, the Second-Waiter, grinning and displaying his dentures, opened the doors and in came the bloods making their way to their tables. All attentive and bold bonhomie, the wingers began pulling out chairs, flicking out napkins and filling tumblers from large silver water jugs. The murmur of voices, the tinkle of glassware and cutlery had increased in volume as the dining saloon began to fill with hungry and excited passengers. Delicious galley smells from the entree courses, brought in on silver serving dishes, began to assail the saloon.

The minutes ticked by, but no sign yet of the captain and his party. By a quarter to eight the saloon was full of noisy chatter and laughter, crackers were being pulled and paper hats sat upon happy heads, but still no sign of the captain. The tiger, now looking agitated, went over to talk to the headwaiter, who listened, his head nodding, then made a call on the phone just behind the main dummy.

'They're still in his dayroom, drinking,' said the tiger on his return. 'Go and tell the Chef that the Old Man isn't down yet and can he make sure that there'll be enough smoked salmon left, enough for eight.'

Go and tell the Chef! Me tell the Chef? I don't think so. No-one ever 'told' him anything as he always seemed to have a meat cleaver in his hand - I knew that much. Being of Italian extraction and therefore excitable, he might be inclined to throw a wobbly. I approached with deference and tact, but it didn't work. He really went into one, but then any request made of him (like most of the chefs you're likely to meet at sea or on shore) without about three days' notice was enough for him to approach melt-down. It must be their temperament or part of their training.

'No, no, no Luigi. Watch Paolo and try it again, this time louder and with more passion. Ready, head up... Look at the ceiling and higher with the hands and the cleaver, shake it, all together now: MAMMA MIA!'

When I got back the tiger was in a panic, trying to pull two chairs out together, trying to seat two ladies at once, a bit like musical chairs. The Old Man's party had arrived, making an entrance, all jolly and noisy. The men were in evening dress, the ladies in gowns and jewellery. When we had them seated I went around with the water jug, removing the napkin from each tumbler and handing it to Sir or Madam before pouring. By the time the tiger had taken their orders for starters most of the other diners were beginning their main courses. It made him feel up the wall straight away and put him out of synch with the progress of the serving of the meal in the galley. It put me on the defensive when at the press asking for anything, as if the galley crowd were blaming me for being late. Some of the tiger's nervousness was beginning to infect me.

They had progressed through the starters – there hadn't been a problem over the smoked salmon, there'd been enough for everyone. Just as I was going around the table, intent on topping up any tumblers and removing cutlery that had become redundant, the incident happened.

'...getting in, what?' The voice was cut glass, educated, full of good breeding and if you paid attention to what was being said you could learn a thing or two. There seemed to be a silence, then I realized with a heart stopping shock that everyone, even the Old Man, was looking expectantly at me. I completely froze; my mouth had gone dry. Had I done something wrong? The tiger too was looking at me, his face a mask of consternation. Christ!

'I said, young man, you must be looking forward to getting in, what?' It was the matronly lady with the black shawl and pearl earrings, swung right around in her seat and peering up at me through a pair of spectacles held on a slim handle that I had only ever seen in the pictures. She had a quizzical, almost offended look on her puffy pink features.

'Oh me! Oh, yes! Oh, sorry! Yes, yes I am...very much, Madam.' I faltered and fell over the words, trying to get them around what felt like a soup ladle in my mouth, heartily agreeing with her, nodding and grinning; going right over the top to assure her, to assure the table, the Captain, the tiger, the headwaiter – even the chef in the galley – that I, the humble *commis*, hadn't been snubbing her and 'Yes, yes I was looking forward to getting in.'

Bloody hell! I just hadn't expected any of them to actually talk to me, to ask me a question other than a query concerning the menu. Perhaps the tiger should have warned me or maybe I should have been wearing a notice around my neck with *'Dummy, nil by mouth'* printed on it. My ears were burning and I was conscious of the Old Man giving me curious looks for the duration of the meal. The incident left me red in the face and destroyed what self-confidence I had right through the main course, and I was still feeling shaky going out to get desserts nearly an hour later. When eventually I got below and took off my jacket, my T shirt beneath was soaking and all because of what? Because for a very minor moment, a kindly matron, perhaps noticing my nervousness and how young I was, had sought to speak to me. Her action had opened the shutters on a spotlight and had put me centre stage, had allowed my betters to peer at me. I was finding out a few things about myself, becoming ultra self-conscious.

Not that I would have been able to explain or admit to my fear of being in contact with the middle or upper classes then, or even until later in life. I knew I could not articulate my opinions or sustain a serious conversation with such people but having a role to hide behind helped. It was only years later, when I had matured enough and developed a degree of confidence that I could relate to those who had received a better education. Blessed with a curiosity of the world I would one day become a reader and increase my cultural awareness; music, literature and language and just how much a voyage - the sea - and those who travel upon it –is a metaphor for life. From Homer's *Odyssey* through the *Ship of Fools* to *The Caine Mutiny*, men and women have been 'finding out a few things about themselves'. Perhaps one of the greatest sea stories has to be Melville's *Billy Budd*, which concerns itself with, among other themes, the individual and how he relates to society. At the time though, I really was something of a raw prawn.

Perhaps not quite what Melville had in mind, but my attempt to relate to society up on the Captain's table had been a disaster and it caused me a degree of humiliation. My maiden voyage had been the final breaking of a boy, the moulding of a youth, and now this, my second trip had been another step in my rites of passage.

***

Thunk! Thunk - thunk! Tiny was at it again, trying for the double twenty, striding back and forth to the dartboard during our supper. As a result of his activity there were certain seats that no one sat in for fear of getting a bounced dart in the neck.

'Excuse me, would you mind not throwing darts whilst we're dining,' said a mild voice. Those of us who heard it looked up in surprise. It was Cyril, a skinny winger who wore glasses and kept himself to himself, usually with his head in a book. Tiny didn't respond immediately, although he may have been expecting a protest. Returning from the board, darts in a meaty fist, he towered over the slight figure of Cyril, who happened to be sat near the danger zone.

'What you going to do about it, you little prick?' he said in a loud and threatening voice. It caused the rest of us, busy eating our supper, to look up and take an interest. Skinny Cyril having a go at Tiny? Blimey!

'I'm merely asking that you desist from throwing darts whilst we dine. It's not right,' replied Cyril.

'Merely asking are you...?' began Tiny, speaking in a namby pamby way. Before he could continue, however, an older, bald-headed man known as Vince was on his feet. He was the bloke from the plate-house and until then had maintained a low profile.

'He's right, I think you ought to pack it in whilst we're eating,' he said loudly.Others by now were taking an interest and some were beginning to stand in support. Tiny glared about him and then with one movement, hurled the three darts at the board. He seemed to swell and get even bigger. Red in the face he glared about him like a buffalo trapped in an airing cupboard and I felt a scare go through me as his eye caught mine; then swinging back to Cyril, who was now also on his feet, he said, 'I'm gonna bleedin' 'ave you, you four-eyed prat,' pushing his big face into Cyril's.

No one said a word and time seemed to stop before Tiny stormed out, kicking a chair out of his way. A collective release seemed to sigh through us and the meal resumed, but we had somehow – all of us in the mess-room – achieved a sense of solidarity, and a wave of respect went out to Skinny Cyril and Vince. It was only later Steve noticed that of Tiny's three hurled darts, two were in the double twenty at the top of the board.

Peter Joseph Troy

Below Decks

Wellington

At about eight o'clock on a sunny but chill autumnal morning in late April we steamed into Wellington harbour. The stiff breezes funnelling through the Cook Straits blew away the remaining humid airs that had lain trapped throughout the vessel since Panama and invigorated everyone with a renewed sense of purpose. It wheeled the hungry gulls about the bay, their cries in our wake seeming to herald our arrival. The continual hoot and bleat of the surrounding tugs as they nudged us into position and the answering tinkle of the bridge telegraph helped to evaporate any residual listlessness amongst the crew.

Everyone had been up and about since daybreak. The passengers, all warmly dressed in their going-ashore clothes, looked overdressed and somewhat formal, their holiday wear along with photos, souvenirs and gifts now packed away in their luggage ready for customs. A real buzz of excitement was evident as those up on deck lined the rails, some peering through binoculars as they tried to spot family and friends amongst the distant throng of people waiting on the quay to which we were making a slow but steady approach.

Breakfast was early because of our imminent arrival. The distinctive smell of kippers pervaded the vessel and carried with it a redolence of dark and foggy London teatimes. A reminder that, without leaving the planet, we were about as far from home as it's possible to get, and I wondered about Mum and Rosie and what they were doing. It would be evening in England, probably cold and wet. They might even be having kippers for tea, or had they already left? There might be a letter for me when we got in.

The wingers, standing by and ready to serve those passengers who appeared for this, their final meal on board, were huddled in small groups peering through the port-holes of the saloon, taking note of what British vessels were berthed and visible from their ever changing view of the harbour.

'Look, – on Queens. It's the bloody *Wanganella*!

'Not the old iron lung - did I ever tell you about...?

'Tell Scouse in the pantry that the *Port Townsend*'s in. His brother's on it.'

'What's that Star boat? Is it the *Dunedin Star*?'

'It's the D.M! And she's getting up steam.'

M.V. Dominion Monarch

Steve came down into the saloon, his hair blown all about. I'd been covering for him in case his bloods had come in, but they hadn't. We'd been taking it in turns to have a look on the deck above and as none of my crowd was in yet I nipped up again to have another look. We were now much closer in and there were many passengers on this, the starboard side of the vessel, as it became increasingly obvious that we were going to berth this side on. The morning, although still bright, had begun to cloud over now and then, as the freshening breeze blew low and ragged clouds rapidly southward. Gale force gusts threatened to whisk away the hats of those who hadn't removed them or weren't clamping them to their heads with a firm hand. The passengers, now in a jolly and expectant mood, appeared to enjoy these sudden gusts, laughing as each one occurred whilst they peered and scanned the faces of the crowd on the quay which had swollen in number. Handkerchiefs were being waved and a sign was raised on which large red letters said: 'WELCOME HOME KAREN'. A chunky looking man with a beard and wearing a tartan shirt had a child on his shoulders. A sudden break in the cloud and a shaft of sunlight brightened the child's golden hair as she waved wildly with both arms.

Behind the crowd on the quay lay sheds and warehouses, and further back in the hills houses and flats were sited at different levels amongst trees and foliage, an occasional window glinting. A cable car ascended slowly and steeply from behind office roofs and buildings. Wellington was getting up: another day beginning.

A lady passenger's white-gloved hand near the rail suddenly shot up, waving frantically and a squeal of pleasure erupted as a daughter, sister or a niece was recognised. 'Julia! Juuulia! Look, look, in the straw hat. It's Julia! Hasn't she grown?' As we got nearer to the quay, more and more hands began to shoot up, hankies and headscarves waving frantically. Men, women and children began calling and squealing in breathless, sobby voices, laughing and crying all at once. Streamers snaked from ship to shore, from shore to ship, so many in fact that they almost rendered the mooring lines unnecessary. Shipping company and customs personnel, some in blue uniforms, others in boiler suits or civvies, were taking up positions, ready with gangways and barriers. We were in.

The breakfasts taken that morning were little more than brief snacks taken on the run as the excited passengers hurried to disembark, to get through customs and to be on their way. Those who hadn't tipped their stewards (and didn't intend to walk out on them) did so now. I found it difficult and embarrassing trying to reconcile my expectation of a tip with a seemingly surprised and grateful demeanour as Neil's mother passed me an envelope, which I gratefully received without having any idea of what it contained. There were lots of fond goodbyes and waves from the children and suddenly, so suddenly the children's dining saloon was empty and barren, the high-chairs forlorn as if the Pied Piper had played upon his pipe and charmed the children away. All that was left as evidence of them, apart from the remains of the breakfast, was one broken red plastic fire engine. Who did they grow up to be?

By eleven o'clock the used tablecloths and napkins had been bagged and were outside the linen locker, ready for the laundry ashore. The main dining saloon and public areas had been swept, scrubbed and polished, and all brass was gleaming. Apart from about four or five tables which had been set for lunch, at which officers and officials would dine whilst we were in port, the rest had had their chairs upended and set upon them. New working schedules had been set up and I had been allocated the morning telephone watch for the remainder of the week.

Wellington became the capital of New Zealand less than 100 years earlier in 1865. It has a natural harbour and its location on the south-western tip of the North Island allows easy access, via ferries, to the South Island. Since the 1840s it was the port that defined the town and by 1850 its population had grown to over 5000. Shipping in 1955 was still the main source of employment for its citizens. Smartly uniformed naval and customs officers, stout and bearded seamen, stevedores, drivers, warehouse and office personnel, typists and filing clerks: all were doing their bit in assisting the movement of cargo from and to all parts of the globe, whether such cargo was human, animal, vegetable or mineral. It might be the new Presbyterian minister, the very Reverent Hamish McPhee, arriving back from a sabbatical in Ayrshire and travelling down to Dunedin to take up a new position at St Andrews. It could be several hundred tons of lamp-black, now being unloaded at Aotea wharf. Whatever it was gave all employees and many others – barmen, taxi drivers, prostitutes, the police – something in common: shipping! It seemed to unite and provide a focus to everything about Wellington.

Although deemed to be a city (it had a city council), this very cohesion and its small scale in comparison with the only other city that I had experience of – London – would make the place seem town-like and more user-friendly when I came to know it. If Chicago, known as the Windy City and the third largest city in America with a population exceeding three million, could be Sinatra's 'kind of town', then Wellington, also known as a windy city, with its ten square miles and a population of only half a million, was about to become mine. I had no way of knowing at the time of course but Wellington was to feature very prominently in my future. It was astrologically cast that several years hence I would pay its rates, use its library, its transport system, its sewers and drains. A crystal ball might have told that a time would come when I would work its waterfront 'standing on the corner', ready to load cargoes of wool, lamb and apples. One day I would walk its hills with a mailbag, and eventually survey with theodolite and chain its surrounding bush. Tea leaves may have predicted the golden times and wedding bells ahead, but as I stood that first morning on the deck of the *Ruahine* how could I have known? Shipping back then was Wellington; I was arriving on a ship, nearly twelve thousand miles from London, and it felt like coming home.

It was whilst I was on telephone watch that Gallagher came up and gave me my letter from Mum. It wasn't a blue aerogramme, but an envelope stuffed with news. She had been accepted and sponsored by Mr Coleman on his sheep station. There were berths still available on a ship called the *Rangitiki* as some who had been scheduled to sail had had second thoughts about emigration to the other side of the world. Who could blame them as many who made the journey during the fifties never expected being able to return to Britain? Flights were out of the question on grounds of cost, and even the fare back by sea cost an arm and a leg. Mum's letter contained details of the sailing itinerary, which gave dates and ports at which the *Rangitiki* would be calling. The dates of course were different but the ports were identical to ours. It seemed unbelievable that in a few short weeks Mum and Rosie would be here: here in Wellington! So much had happened in my life in such a brief period that I was experiencing some sort of over-load and felt that time was playing tricks on me.

'Hello! Motor Vessel *Ruahine* here, can I help you?' It was the following morning and I was back in my Buttons outfit (minus the pillbox). I was on telephone duty and this was a call for the third engineer, Andy Anderson. 'Hang on please; I'll see if he's on board. Can I take your name and number in case we get cut off?' I made a note and went off in search of Anderson.

It was a woman on the phone, the line squeezing her Kiwi vowels, making them sound shrill and tinny. 'Till him it's Brinda. Hi'll know.'

He wasn't in his cabin and his bunk looked as if it hadn't been slept in. I looked into the engineers' mess and asked a couple of his mates who were dawdling over the remains of a late breakfast, their cigarettes and coffee-pot before them.

'Who wants him, man?' said one with a Geordie accent.

'A bird called Brenda,' I told him.

'Don't they all,' sniggered the other, shaking his head.

'Tell her he's on watch and he'll phone her later,' said the Geordie.

When I got back several minutes later, Brenda was still hanging on and I passed on the message. 'Will youse pleese till him I rung and be sure he's got my number?' she asked.

The phone call was typical of the many that I took when on phone duty. Brenda rang several times, each time the note of desperation and disappointment in her voice a touch more acute, but I don't think Anderson ever got back to her. After about a week of phone duty you didn't have to be a candidate for the Samaritans to divine what dramas were going on in the lives of numerous callers, the majority of them women.

***

'The prennial question? Well if you don't know it, son, how can you ask it?'

'You can't.'

'So what is the prennial question then?'

'It's not prennial, it's p<u>e</u>rennial and yes I know what it is and I can ask it.'

'Well ask it then.'

'Yes, but who do I ask?'

'Well ask me, sunshine, and if I know the answer I'll tell you.'

'You won't know the answer. No-one on this ship does.'

'Well for Chris-sake ask me and let me be the judge of that.'

I was ear-wigging in on their chat in the plate-house, silver-dipping cutlery and cruets. Skinny Cyril and Vince the plate-man were into one of their complicated debates, which I found interesting but wouldn't have known how to join. Despite their age difference, almost twenty years at a guess, and their obviously different educational and social backgrounds, they'd both become matey since the Tiny episode in the mess. They were both loners and each seemed to be content to have his head in a book. Vince was reading his way through Dennis Wheatley (I had read one of his called *The Devil Rides Out* and a rattling good tale it was). Skinny Cyril was into a book called *The Outsider*, which I had looked at in the crew library but had had difficulty with what the author was on about.

'All right,' said Skinny Cyril, 'I'll ask you, but you won't know. What, in your opinion, is enlightenment?'

'Jesus, is that all? To be enlightened means to be told how to do something. When I first came into this plate-house I had to be shown how to operate this machine. I became enlightened, didn't I.' Vince was amused by the whole thing. 'Christ, anyone can tell you that, even that prat Tiny.'

'The word has different meanings,' said Skinny Cyril. 'All you've accomplished is to give me the basic dictionary definition.'

'Oh do me a favour, piss off!' laughed Vince.

But I knew that they'd be at it again, either later in the mess or ashore. Whether or not it was as a result of them being seen together, Tiny's threats had so far come to nothing. You could tell though, if you had half an eye, that Vince had a hard on for

Tiny and was looking for a way to provoke him, and I wanted to be there when it happened. Tiny was a bruiser, bigger, younger and stronger but my money'd be on Vince. There wasn't a lot to him but he was wiry, had a repressed violence and I got the impression he'd enjoyed many a scrap. His nose wasn't broken but had a definite starboard list and a few of his teeth were missing. There was also a sort of concavity to his features as if a vacuum had occurred within his head. But what really would make you wary of him were his eyes. There was wildness in them, and with the prominent set of his chin he came over as totally reckless.

***

The Florida Milk Bar on Lambton Quay smelt of boiled and burnt milk, and it was there that I began to hang out with the other boy-ratings when not on board. There were plenty of bars and hotels if you wanted to drink something stronger and, although being under age, on occasion we did, nursing a jug of D.B. Lager between four and just watching the changing scene in De-Brett's Lounge Bar, or upstairs in The Duke of Edinburgh. It was the Florida that claimed our attention and custom, however, and not just because of the boiled milk. At about four o'clock the place would begin to fill with sixth-form girls from the local college and their school uniforms were definitely something of a turn-on. They were of the Ronald Searle variety, the girls and the uniforms: tall, leggy, black-stockinged and saucy just like their screen sisters, the girls of St Trinian's. Fortunately for us our image seemed to be as attractive to them as theirs was to us, for the clothing styles in New Zealand at that time for both sexes were very dowdy. Fashion was several years behind the UK and the sight of a bloke even a bit Teddish attracted the most admiring glances from the Kiwi girls. No wonder that Spider had developed such a technique with his Brylcreem and his barnet.

The Kiwi male didn't offer too much competition, well not in the Florida anyhow. Given the lack of fashionable clothing plus the fact that there weren't any decent men's hairdressers in Wellington, he didn't stand a chance. His 'short back and sides' was so severe that the average Ted would only need one about once a year (Mr Reed would have approved).

Our Kiwi brethren were also under another disadvantage when it came to the pull. To be in the Florida at that time of day he would probably be a schoolboy and as such it was compulsory for him to wear school uniform. As most of the lads were enormous, to see one of them of over six foot dressed in short grey trousers and with a ridiculous cap upon his head, well he didn't stand a chance and definitely gave us the edge. Given their start in life, however, and the benefit of a sound education, I'm sure that those self same boys with their satchels and books went on to make something of themselves: perhaps eventually becoming All Blacks, dentists or politicians. At the time, however, we were streets ahead with our blue suede brothel creepers and drainpipe pants; and subsequently all the way into the warm embraces of the St. Trinian's mob. They fell for us, we were 'Pommy jokers' from the Old Country, men of the world and we had style. We brought close for these young women their own heritage. Many had grandparents, if not parents, who came from Britain and one day they themselves were going to make the trip. It was to be - as the man said - 'like taking candy from a baby.'

'Inny one of youse jokers from London?' She was beside our table, a precocious and full-figured girl, her hair in pigtails.

'J...Joe is,' volunteered Gallagher, sitting opposite. We were sitting in one of the booths in the Florida and by now, after several days, had become a familiar sight in there. She slid in beside me, her stocking-clad legs making a gentle ziss on the orange Rexene of the seat, and turning her hazel eyes into mine, she asked, 'Do youse know a Kinny Hirris? He lives in London.'

For a moment there she had me, was she kidding? But no, she seemed excited and was off nineteen-to-the-dozen.

'He's my cousin and lives in Maple Road, number fourteen and just started work in an insurance office and he's got a dog called Rix and...and... oh yes, he's tall with dark hair and goes on holidays in Bongar or Boggar or somewhere like that and, and...'

She was so excited, almost willing me to say I knew him, and I felt as if I was letting her down by not doing so. I sat and listened and drank her in. So did Gallagher, both of us throwing in the odd nod, occasionally saying yes when we could get a word in. With her pigtails, held by rubber bands, and her healthy vitality washing over us both, she burbled and fizzed along. It was something new for me seeing a stunning young woman so animated that I wanted to keep her talking for as long as possible, as she rattled away giving more clues, hoping that we might know him. There was something so touchingly naïve and innocent about her (such as believing London to be no larger than Wellington) that I craftily began to think of ways that I might see her again - but without Gallagher.

'Do you have a photo of him?' I asked when she paused to draw breath.

'Oh yis. I can meet youse both here tomorrow and I'll bring it with me.'

I could tell that if I didn't become slippery then Gallagher, being Gallagher, would goose-gog along and might even bring Steve and Leo along. I had to get rid of him briefly so suggested that he might like to buy her a milkshake. He was back shortly with a strawberry one. Time enough though for me to find out that she lived up in Kelburn - top of the cable car, its entrance a few steps from the Florida, and I arranged to meet her there privately at four o'clock the following day.

It worked. It was my first 'pick-up' and proved to be my neatest ever. We didn't pore over Kinny's photo too long and what she taught me in the Botanical Gardens had little to do with botany, although she might have gone on to major in anatomy. Yes, I had kissed a girl before but Elsie Brier's kisses hadn't been anything like kissing her. In comparison, kissing Elsie had been like kissing Aunt Lil's budgie.

Perhaps it was different here in the Southern Hemisphere; maybe the girls matured quicker or could it be something in the water? Whatever it was, Marie's kisses drove me wild. Our snogging sessions seemed to go on for ages and time began to behave differently, an hour seeming like ten minutes. To fondle a healthy young woman was so exciting, but we never went all the way. Why? Well of course where could we go to do the deed, and just as things were getting torrid she would hesitate enough for me to remind myself that I was the man-of-the-world and she a schoolgirl. It was, after all, the mid fifties and social mores were then quite different. Besides, I had a younger sister about her age and although I wouldn't have been 'Broaching the Cargo' there did exist a law called 'Carnal Knowledge'. It wasn't long before parental authority became aware and she never appeared in the Florida again. Phew! With one bound I was free.

***

The second letter that I received from Mum was brief and just to tell me that everything had gone to plan. She and Rosie would be sailing on the *Rangitiki* and would be arriving here in Wellington in late June, a date unfortunately that would find me homeward bound. Immigration officials would be meeting her on arrival and arranging transport for them to Masterton. I would, of course, try to get up to see them as I intended to make another trip on the *Ruahine*, hopefully taking leave and spending time with them at the sheep station.

At seventeen (and a half), my life had taken on new dimensions and I was brimming with new experiences and adventures. Mum and Rosie were yesterday, symbols of domesticity and childhood, and of course I loved them but, but... the truth was that I had said goodbye. I had flown the coop, skedaddled. I had somehow got an early start on life. Life was out there, or rather here on this ship or another. All I had to do was turn-to when called and this or a similar ship would show me the world.

From a deck of cards I had been dealt a hand, and as I didn't fully understand the rules of the game I had no way of knowing if the cards I was holding made a good hand or not. All I could do is what anyone can do and that is to play them, only recognizing the foolish or wise play for what it was at a much later date. It's a complicated game, too, because yesterday's play may look foolish today; but then with hindsight, a month or two later it could appear wise. It's a belief that I still have nearly sixty years later, and the game is still in progress. Translated, it could be stated as *'Be careful for what you wish for.'*

The ship spent several weeks on the coast and we all took advantage of it: beaches, cinemas, dances, hotel lounge bars, grotty pubs, even parties where all that was required was a trip to the bottle store before the shutters came down at six o'clock. New Zealand was dry after six and the hour before was known as the swill hour. Having shut up shop or office at five, or (perish the thought) at half past, workers would crowd into lounges and bars to get the grog down them. The Duke of Edinburgh pub had its own degree of grottiness; civic-minded citizens were reputed to wipe their feet on the mat *before* leaving it and stepping out onto the pavement.

There were of course no drink drive laws in those days so after six o'clock you had to be extra careful crossing the road. Attempting to cross Willis Street was a bit like stepping out onto the track at Silverstone. Buses were packed and standing in a taxi queue to make it out to a suburb like Berhampore with your entrance fee (six bottles of Steinlager or DB lager) to a party that you'd heard about in the pub could be an interesting experience. Two or three of us would stand patiently in line for the next available cab when two old biddies in front of us who didn't want to lose their place in the queue would need to get rid of several schooners of lager consumed earlier. We learnt to avert our gaze and hide our amusement as they took it in turns to perch over the kerb to pee.

Those of the crew in the know managed to get casual labour on the waterfront during the afternoon or early evening (known as 'sea-gulling'), because after about mid-day most chores for the day on board ship had been done. It was well paid work and in-hand too, so it meant you didn't have to apply for a sub out of your wages once a week.

'I met her outside the Embassy Cinema,' said Steve, 'that one I was dancing with in the Trades Hall on Wednesday night, and she slipped me a ten bob note to take her in, stuffed it into my top pocket she did.' The New Zealand women were very aware that our wages were less than half of theirs and it was usual on meeting up for a date for us to be subbed by them. Did we have it made or did we have it made?

***

The ship, still in Wellington, has moved berth, and we're now tied up on Aotea Quay, which is not so handy for just nipping ashore and several of us are sprawled aft on deck after lunch with our shirts off, trying to top up our bronzy. The heat of summer has passed but the sun is quite hot and the wind has dropped.

'Are we still evolving?' Skinny Cyril wants to know but now we're calling him Cy. With mugs of tea he and Vince are seated on the edge of the hatch to number four hold, which won't be opened until we arrive in Lyttelton.

'Yeah, as a species I reckon we are,' replies Vince, 'although I don't know about Tiny. You reckon we are?'

'Oh most definitely, Vincent, of course we are,' goes Cy with his perfectly modulated English voice. 'Not to evolve means there can be no progress for the human race, and if so what's the point of it all? And it's not just the biological, the Darwinian. Take consciousness for instance. We Homo Sapiens have self-consciousness but animals, from which we have evolved, have only simple consciousness.'

'I thought we were all Homo Erectus, as we get the horn and walk on two legs, don't we?' says Vince. 'What's this Sappy thing?'

'Well we were at one time Homo Erectus but that was thousands of years ago. Since then our species has evolved into Homo Sapiens. We are now physically different, but getting back to consciousness, take that seagull on the rail, it doesn't know it's a seagull, does it?'

'I dunno, if not a seagull who does it think it is then?'

'No, that's the whole point, Vince. It doesn't have any idea of self; it has no way of knowing. It can feel hunger, pain and alarm, but...'

'Oi you two! Fuck off cos we don't want to hear all about your bleedin' homo mates.' Tiny has been lying like an orangutan on the hatch cover and now sitting up he gives them both a volley. It's their talk of homos and his name being mentioned earlier that has wound him up.

'Take no notice of that prat,' says Vince loudly. 'You were talking about animals being simple and one of 'em thought it had the right of reply.' His comment causes a snigger or two, and that is enough. Those who have been dozing stir themselves. Is this it? It seems it is as by now Tiny is on his feet and with a scowl he swings down from off the hatch and confronts Vince.

'Take the piss out of me, would you? Stand up, you berk!'

But Vince doesn't stand up, he's no fool and anyway he's perfectly positioned where he is. With his mug of tea still in hand, he swings his right leg from the knee, almost casually, and plants a well placed boot right into Tiny's nuts. Blink and you'd have missed it. Tiny goes down like the proverbial, moaning and curled up, cupping his balls, his face tight with agony. To see a big bloke like Tiny go down so easily is awesome.

'Where were we?' says Vince into Cy's startled face. 'You were saying...?'

Going South

From Wellington we steamed south to Lyttelton, which is about a third the way down the eastern coast of the South Island and is the main port to Christchurch, where we moored for about ten days. The Canterbury Plains are to the south of Christchurch and their main exports comprised wool, lamb and fruit. One day I would live there too, but that's much later.

It was from Lyttelton that Shackleton set forth for the Antarctic back in 1909 and the name is also reputed to be linked, through an ancestor, to Humphrey Lyttelton, the late jazz musician.

'You coming to the Bake-house Ball tonight, Joe?' It was Johnny Murray.

'I dunno, what is it?' I replied.

'It's a dance above the Baker's shop, just up the street – should be a laugh.'

'Yeah sure, count me in.'

'Starts at eight, so we get there about half past. Okay?'

Every Saturday night the girls came in by train, through the tunnel from Christchurch under the Port hills, to attend. If our clothing was 'with-it' in Wellington, then here in this small port (population approximately 23) we must have appeared to the natives as being right over the top.

It was at the Bake-house Ball that Saturday night that Murray and I both blew it. It was there also that Gallagher, being

Gallagher, blew it as well when he loaned Ken Biggs, another winger, his last half a crown. Biggsy then took Molly home. Gallagher never got his money back as Biggsy was never seen again.

Standing beside Murray in front of adjacent washbasins, both shaving before going ashore again to the Ball the following week, we're planning how the evening might shape up.

'Play it cool, but not too cool as otherwise we'll blow it again,' said Murray. Our memories of the previous week were still raw, as we'd both made mistakes then. By not offering to buy any of the women a coke you'd keep 'em guessing. It wasn't the best ploy if you wanted to score though. What you didn't want to do was to begin to take too much of an interest, for you might see the woman of your dreams come through the door at any moment. If there were rules I wasn't aware of them and women were strange creatures.

'What about those two over there, John; her in the pink and her mate?' I'd said to him last Saturday.

'Well she's all right but I don't like your one. I've seen more meat on a rusty coat-hanger. Nah, it's still early. We'll hang about.' And we did. The last dance, usually a waltz, could be the clincher if you were going to take someone back to their place and hopefully stay for breakfast. Dream on, brother! With an eye on the clock as the dance had begun to wind up we had at last decided to make our move. But that one in the yellow, whom I'd been keeping in reserve, was then smiling and laughing into the eyes of a short tubby bloke with a moustache. Oh well, it'll have to be the skinny one in the pink and with the beehive... where is she? Nope she'd done a runner – gone.

'Ladies and gentlemen, it has been our enormous pleasure to have entertained you this evening,' had said the bloke spinning the discs, 'so will you please take your partners now for the last waltz. Let's have you all on the floor whilst we lower the lights...'

The memory of what followed made me cringe and I was determined that we wouldn't repeat our shameful actions.

'Excuse me, would you like the last dance? No? What d'ya mean no? Well suit yourself, I'm spoilt for choice here...'

'Excuse me, would you...? No? Well what about you then...or even you?'

The desperation was contagious and even Murray had lost it. 'Oi you! D'ya fancy the last waltz? I'll drive you home afterwards. Well no, I don't have a car but I have a bloody great whip. What? Well be like that then.'

That had been last week. This week would be different though, no more cheeky dialogue. Murray and I had talked it through and our ablutions were over.

'Now here's the plan, Troy,' said Murray, slapping on the Old Spice. 'Tonight we go ugly early.'

***

The ship returned to Wellington for another ten days where we took on stores and additional cargo before embarking passengers for the return trip to the UK.

Gallagher had rapidly become the butt of many jokes and stories and coming from Dursley didn't seem to help. He was reputed to be hung like a horse, however, by those who had seen him in the shower.

'Bloody Hell,' said Leo, 'You seen the snake on him? He's got enough there to put a hand-rail round the engine room. He doesn't take it out, he uncoils it.'

Gallagher's clothes when going ashore... well he didn't exactly have style: a wrinkled shirt and an old olive green cardigan that might have been his dad's seemed to be the only clobber he had, plus his saloon blues and black brogue shoes. He'd even been in front of the Second Steward for having holes in his socks when on duty. 'Did you hear the one about Gallagher?' was often the opening line to a funny story, and he was often the target for any wind up. I suppose in every school, workplace or institution there will always be a Gallagher, and those who will exploit them. Someone, it might have been Steve, came up with the idea that we'd get more mileage out of him if we put it about that a real honey of a woman had the hots for him.

The Florida Milk Bar in Lambton Quay wasn't the only place in town where we'd hang out. Sammy's in Manners Street, nearly opposite the Duke of Edinburgh pub up on the corner where the trams hung a left on their way to Courtenay Place, also served boiled milk and although it didn't have the St Trinian's mob in there its big attraction was the sweetheart serving: a real doll with a sunny smile and big blue eyes plus a mass of thick straw-coloured hair. Although she wore an apron there was evidence of ample breasts as well. She was of that type that her beauty could take your breath away but she seemed way out of our reach. She was at a guess a good ten years older than us, maybe even pushing thirty. All of us had been in there to ogle her over a milkshake.

'Listen, Gallagher, do yourself a favour. Wake up. Can't you see she's nutty about you...she can't seem to take her eyes of you.' We were on the tram, jolting along Lambton Quay, heading back towards the wharf when we began winding him up.

'You lucky bastard...Christ if I had half the chance...'

'You have got to get in there, sunshine...'

'Some older women really like a bit of young.'

To be the focus of such attention caused Gallagher a lot of embarrassment and we didn't let up until he'd promised us that he would attempt to chat her up.

'Y-You really thi-think so?' Gallagher would manage to stammer shyly many times. 'H-Honestly?'

Part one of the wind up was in place. Part two required that we should prepare him to win her heart and be there to witness his attempt. The following afternoon we had him all dogged up in borrowed gear. Leo had loaned him his hounds-tooth jacket with the velvet collar, which Gallagher could get into but couldn't button. It didn't matter because the green silk tie with a yellow parrot on it, loaned from Steve, would be hugely prominent, its Windsor knot hiding the missing button from my Rael Brook drip-dry shirt with the cut-away collar and French cuffs. We also got him into a pair of drainpipe pants and suede brothel creepers, borrowed from one of the wingers.

'Just go up to her when she isn't serving and ask if she'll meet you tonight,' Leo was busy rehearsing him for the about tenth time. And that's just what Gallagher did, about an hour later, when several of us sat in two booths to witness the event. Leo gave him the go-ahead when the time was right, so he slouched over to the counter, as we nudged one another and drank in every moment until...

'Thank you so much for asking,' she replied to his awkward request. She came from around the counter and beamed at him all blue eyes and white teeth. 'My name is Samantha, and you? You are?' He managed to get his name out before she said, 'I'd love to see *'Oklahoma'*. It's on at the Embassy. We could go tonight?' He came back to us embarrassed with success.

'Sh, sh, she wants me to, to call back for her at, at, s,s,seven, w,w, what d, do I do now?'

We all waited up for him like anxious parents that night, but Gallagher never got back. He arrived much later the following morning, looking shagged out, missed a lifeboat drill and got logged a day's pay. But after that Samantha (she owned the place) made sure he wasn't late again by paying for a cab for him every morning thereafter until we sailed from Wellington.

Okay, he seemed exhausted and often dozed when on telephone duty, but he didn't complain and even began to lose his stammer. She kept him well fed on a special diet and sat him at a special table she'd set up for him at the rear of her milk bar. We'd see him through the window, getting plenty of protein, steak, eggs, and even oysters. She took charge of him, bought him new clobber and made a real fuss over him. He wouldn't give us any details when asked how Sammy 'performed' but just blushed. We all ate our hearts out, of course, and some tried it on with her. It didn't get any of us anywhere as she only had eyes for her 'Galahad', as she called him, making him promise to return next trip.

Peter Joseph Troy

***

I made numerous trips to New Zealand over several years, and can't always remember which vessel I was aboard when certain incidents happened. But I realized even then they were my salad days as adolescence carried me forward into manhood.

In the photo that was taken in 1959, at the top of Queen Street in Auckland, I'm standing outside a bank with a group dressed in the mandatory wranglers of the day. John Murray's up front, he's moved on having set the trend and looks as though he's the manager of our pop group, and he could have been too. Tal Carrol is the tall guy on the right and was a superb guitarist. The James Dean look-alike (extreme left) is Mick Abbot and Dave Driver's head peers from the back. There's Garry, whose surname I forget and that's me carrying the amp. I've lost touch with them all except John Murray who, at 73, now lives in Australia and still goes to sea.

The following incident must have occurred when I had become more mature and thus more confident and understanding of how to impress a woman. There were then those women who, when I was conversing with them, gave me their full attention; others constantly let their eyes drift away over my shoulder to see who was coming through the door and were easily distracted from my riveting persona. Some action such as a drive-by-shooting or a chandelier crashing down attracted their attention and they'd lose the plot. Okay, okay it's just feasible that West-Ham coming top of the second division bored them or they did not share my intellectual analysis of certain films.

Pamela wasn't like that, not like that at all. She was an older, much more mature and therefore a more patient woman. She was taller than me in her high heels, which I found something of a turn on and I became aware that if I was to have any chance at all of seducing her I'd have to raise my game.

With her feline eyes full on my face as I explained to her the plotline of 'Ice Cold in Alex', she let them rove over my features, halting for a moment on my lips where they became focused and imploring. It's so exciting for a man to have such attention from a beautiful woman and my loins were all of a tingle, a fact she may well have been aware of as we'd danced through a smoochy slow waltz or two.

I'd just got to that bit in the film where Sylvia Sims lets the ambulance roll back down a sand dune, after they'd all spent the whole morning getting it to the top, when Pamela suggested I might like to see her home, to her flat in Island Bay without waiting for the last waltz. A swift taxi took us, and I got a clue that it wouldn't just be a quick clinch outside her front door when she led me by the hand through it.

It is of course one thing to hold a mature woman's interest in sport or film when you're both in a busy ballroom, but how you got around to what was really on both your minds when behind a locked door is something else, and I was just explaining to her how, in the film, Harry Andrews had suggested that by removing the spark plugs to reduce engine compression and putting the ambulance in reverse it was possible to wind it upwards and backwards with the starting handle, when she took off her blouse and bra.

Never slow on the uptake I became instantly alert, realising her interest in the film had become secondary. I got another clue when she began to unbutton my flies before putting her arms about me and putting her full lips to mine. She seemed a real expert at the kissing business too, her lips parting, then a quick darting of her tongue so that the tumescence that had held me for over an hour now seemed to become a third leg.

Removing her skirt, she straddled me on her sofa so I shut right up about the film realising, that if I played my cards right, I just might be in there. But then, breathing heavily, she paused and looked beseechingly into my eyes.

'I really have a woman's needs, Joe, but I'm petrified about disease. I know that you seamen visit brothels, be truthful and tell me now, do you have anything?'

'No I don't,' I honestly told her.

'Be honest with me, Joe, you'd tell me if you had, wouldn't you?'

She seemed relieved when I nodded, and told me that she had some in the bathroom cabinet. It was a moment of confusion for me, but then the penny dropped.

Suddenly I liked her immensely and wondered if this was love because my heart was going like mad. It wasn't my first time but anything before that became eclipsed by what Pamela had in mind. We had time, privacy and a big bed but more than that she was so demanding and uninhibited. Still wearing her high heels she spurred my bare buttocks; mount and rider were as one as she urged me over the jumps with whimpers and cries. She seemed more than just happy not only with my eagerness to learn, but also my ability to repeat again and again what she was teaching me so that we won many races before dawn arrived.

Much later when we were both sated she told me her story. She had been married at eighteen - over ten years earlier - because she'd then been pregnant. The child had been stillborn and her husband's drinking had got out of control. They were now separated and he'd moved back to Dunedin. She didn't want another relationship but had decided to enjoy herself and make up for her lost teens. It seemed that my meeting her at the Empress Ballroom was part of her plan to compensate for what she felt she had missed out on.

Although the term had not gained currency, I was her toy boy and we explored many avenues of eroticism over the remaining time I had in Wellington. In town she dressed and looked such a respectable woman when I'd meet her outside the offices of the insurance company in which she worked. When we were in her flat, though, she'd dress down and be cheap and tarty and lewd, and it was these opposite qualities that had me obsessed. There have been other adventures since Pamela but never any quite so erotic, vigorous and demanding. But then I was in my prime, with a libido to match hers, and became addicted to her and wanted her more and more. It was something to do with an older woman taking control and it left me guilt free. It wasn't my fault, was it? An older woman had led me on. I had sinned and exulted in my sin. My obsession with her might have been my undoing for I was becoming possessive toward her, and it was the cause of friction between us. Her appetite for other conquests with young men left me saddened and jealous and after we had thoroughly explored each other and no mystery was left, I was hung out to dry.

(*For those readers who might be interested in the film mentioned above, it ended with John Mills insisting on buying them all an ice cold lager in Alexandria, including one for Anthony Quayle, although they all by now knew he was a German spy.*)

***

The different experiences that make up a life, its highs and lows, the people we meet, whether they are ships that pass in the night or have some permanence in our memories, are what makes us who we are. Okay, maybe I'm stating the obvious or getting carried away with my own reflections but that leads me into another revelation and this time not a woman but a bloke. Shock Horror, what am I about to reveal?

Davey Symes was a bloke no-one could forget. He was an original, a one-off who had his own brand of eccentric humour and chose his moments to reveal it. I knew he was a bit odd from the start. The first time I met him he said to me not 'hello' or 'how you doing mate' but looked at me, shook his head and said 'No, you can't!' I looked at him and he said it again to which I replied 'Yes, I can!' We were then off – can't, can, can't, can, batting the words back and forth like kids until he walked away shaking his head. The trick of it was to remain dead-pan when Dave was near and go along with his absurdities, regardless of what he might dream up. He'd peer round the mess room door and shout 'Ready, Troy? It's my turn,' and he'd start.

'Delco Remy!' and I'd reply 'Battleship!' Then we'd be away together – all nonsense.

'Ear plug!'

'Swan Lake!'

'Battery!'

The trick was to answer with the first thing that came into your head and I could never keep up with him.

'Marmalade!'

'Crown and Anchor!'

'John Wayne'

'Uh…duh! Mmm…mmm!'

'Ha ha got you again, that's seven to me,' and he'd laugh and be gone.

The others in the mess-room were puzzled and asked me to explain the rules of the game but I brushed it away saying that unless they'd ever played three dimensional chess they were unlikely to get it.

I might be onboard or ashore, perhaps in conversation with someone and become aware that Dave was beside and peering into my left ear with a magnifying glass. The correct response, to the bemusement to whomever you were talking to, was to gently place one hand up to cover the unexamined ear and ignore Dave who would then wander away. He was a handsome, intelligent bloke, was faithful to his girl Jerry back in Hillingdon, whom he eventually married and one day way into the future I would become their lodger and even be godfather to their son, Peter.

The nature of absurdity – although Symes and I were unaware of it – was at that time beginning to become a genre with works by Pinter, Becket and others: 'The theatre of the Absurd' would eventually and arguably evolve into what since then has been referred to as *'Post-Modern'*. Dave Symes - whereever you maybe – know that you were one of the *Avant-Garde*.

Eight Bob to Battersea

The *Ruahine* arrived back in London on the 7th of July, and I paid off with more money than I had ever seen before. With overtime and tips I had nearly fifty pounds. The nine large white fivers that I received really felt like money, and were ready to burn a hole in my pocket. My previous pay packets had contained one-pound notes, ten-bob notes and silver; my pay-off from the *Beaverburn* may have contained a white fiver, even two, but to have nine large ones! They crinkled and smelt differently from other notes and seemed to put me in a different league completely. My pay, along with my discharge book, came with a request to tick a form if I wanted to sign on for the next trip, and if so, a date for joining. I ticked the correct column and was told to turn-to at eight in the morning on a date about two weeks hence, ready to work-by until we signed articles and sailed for New Zealand again.

For Customs and Excise reasons, only authorized personnel were allowed on board, and none of the crew was allowed ashore until the ship had been cleared. So up until that time all visitors to the ship including the taxi touts had to be content with trying to arrange business by shouting from the wharf. 'Oi! D'ya wanna cab, son? Where you going? Ow many of you?' Those on board who knew the score had organized their transport long ago, long before Channel Night, and had worked out who was going where, so cab sharing (ideally between four) had been arranged. The Ipswich Lip had sounded Gallagher and me out earlier in the trip and we'd agreed to share with him and a storeman who lived in Wandsworth. It was going to cost me about eight bob to Battersea.

By the time we had finished our chores, been through customs, showered and signed off (we'd been packed since the Azores) the ship had been cleared and was busy with shore-side crews, lots of new faces and odd-bods, so it was wise to be cute about your possessions. If you didn't have a key to your cabin or your locker, which we didn't, then someone kept watch. It was surprising just how close and trusting you became to those who you had met only three months ago, and now they were almost family.

Saying goodbye to those you had become mates with was masked with a rough and ready shoulder-punch or piss-take.

'Don't tell me you're coming back next trip, Troy? You are. Oh Christ!'

If they came back next trip, then you might share a cabin. If they didn't return, well you might have their address, or know they came from somewhere called Bovey Tracey or Cleckheaton. There were those with whom you'd been closer to than brothers but you might never set eyes on them again, or if you did then the years might have changed them beyond recognition. For Londoners, many of us who thought we were 'Jack the lad', it gave us pause for thought. Our country cousins, even Gallagher, could be as fly as any city boy after a trip or two, and a reassessment of respect went out to those who, at one time, we might have been inclined to dismiss for their rural origins.

Perhaps a day would come years later when you might walk in to the Navigator's Den in Cape Town, or a hotel in Zanzibar and there making a fool of himself, with a woman on his knee, was your old mate Bob Munn, whom you'd sailed with on the *Rangitata*, (or was it the *Rangitoto*?) More importantly whose round was it anyway? If you spotted him before he spotted you, then you had a moment in which to wind him up. If it was a hotel, then a quick request to the receptionist to put out an announcement over the public address system: *'Attention, please. Would Mr Robert Munn please come to the reception desk as his wife and family have just arrived.'*

So it was finally goodbye and down the gangway I went, my shoulder bruised with fond farewells and into the cab with those travelling in my direction. Although it was a warm and sunny day everything seemed so dank and dreary as we travelled west along the busy Commercial Road. After New Zealand landscapes and the Pacific, everything seemed so claustrophobic. We went first to Fenchurch Street Station where we said goodbye to the Lip, who was catching the train to Ipswich.

It suddenly seemed very quiet in the cab without him as he and the cabby had been really going at it, discussing first of all the dock strike, which had only recently finished, and then moving on to the subject of our troops in Suez. The cabby, who seemed well informed, kept blaming the 'bloodyyanks' for exerting pressure on 'that toss-pot Eden', who had taken over when Churchill had resigned in April.

Without the Ipswich Lip, the cabby was much calmer, although he tried to get us all at it again as we travelled south across London Bridge, this time on the subject of capital punishment and the forthcoming execution of Ruth Ellis. 'She shot the geyser, she knew the rules: course they should top her!' He spat the words from the side of his mouth and over his shoulder at us. He didn't get a lot of response or argument from the three of us left in the cab, as no one seemed to have strong views on the subject. Gallagher, who was next out of the cab, suggested more than once that he and I share a cabin next trip, an idea I was up for because, not admitting to anything as wimpish as liking the guy, the truth was just that. I did.

Mum's brother, Uncle Dick, and his wife, Aunt Lil, really made me welcome at their house in Beaufoy Road. They had given me the little room at the top of the house, which looked westward out to Clapham Junction and beyond to Wandsworth. The house is no longer there, neither is Beaufoy Road. They had survived the Blitz but couldn't withstand the onslaught of urban renewal, or was it slum clearance when it came in the late sixties? Uncle Dick and Aunt Lil, God bless them, are no more either, but in 1955, and over the next few years they could be found with their adult children, my cousins, at home near the junction of Lavender Hill and Queenstown Road.

For the next seven years it was to become, if not my home, then somewhere to touch base, store my gear and direct mail when I was in London. I'm somewhat ashamed to confess that I took it all very much for granted at the time and didn't fully realize just how lucky I was.

It was to be from Lavender Hill between 1955 and 1961, whenever I was in London, that I began to explore and eventually haunt the West End jazz clubs that had begun to burgeon some years earlier, and were blasting away a revival of traditional New Orleans and mainstream jazz. Cy Laurie's, just across from the Windmill and on the edge of Soho, the 100 Club (better known as Humph's, to the Bohemians) and Ken Colyer's, at the 51 club; it was in these three basement clubs that I spent most of my London nights when on leave. The sounds that the bands blew were not so much music to me as a food that seemed to nourish a deep and needy hunger for rhythm.

They were dark and sweaty dives where strangers called you 'Man' and smiled as you 'dug' the beat and got 'gone', your finger's snapping, your head nodding and your eyes closed blissfully as you disappeared head-first into Barber's trombone. George Melly would perform, singing 'Frankie and Johnny were Lovers', making obscene gestures with the microphone before finally acting out 'Bang bang, she shot her man' by falling flat on to the stage with a trembling of his heels. Mysterious yet friendly student-talent got down there, wearing long and heavy sweaters that smelt of musk and fresh armpit, their hair waist-length. I discovered some nifty footwork and found I could jive fast. It wasn't something that you had to learn, you just let yourself go and the music power-drived through you, not leaving you tired but revitalized and firing on all cylinders.

The music seemed to vent any male competitive hostility that was often encountered in dance halls like the Locarno in

Streatham or the Lyceum in the Strand. In all the trad-jazz clubs I ever went to, never did I witness any trouble; everybody seemed to be too intent on really having a good time. It was different in the clubs that played modern jazz. These clubs seemed to attract a more edgy and up-tight crowd who conformed by dressing like the Krays. There was a protocol to observe so if I was going to the Marquee or the Whisky-A-Gogo, which I did in the late fifties, then I would wear a suit and my tie would have a small knot. If I danced I didn't do so in a fast manner but kept cool and somewhat reserved and never, unless you were really looking for 'bovver', did you ask a woman to dance if there was the slightest chance that she was with someone. It was better to go to a modern jazz club with a mate or mob-handed if you weren't taking a girl along. Going on your own could be an empty experience unless of course you really were deeply into the sounds of Dankworth or Zoot Sims, or got off on college-boy haircuts.

When I was in London between those years I became a 'poser', almost a Walter Mitty character. I tried on many uniforms, progressing from Teddy Boy to Bohemian to Mod, then Rocker and in 1961, before I took a one-way trip to live in New Zealand, I got into the Italian gear complete with dark glasses – all in a desperate attempt to attract a girlfriend. You might have found me in shades, attempting to look as intellectual and mysterious as possible and loitering in a coffee bar called The Gyre and Gimbal in John Adam Street, just off the top of Villiers Street at Charing Cross. To complete the effect I would have some suitable paperback with me, perhaps Colin Wilson's *Outsider* or something with Zen in the title. Slowly – very slowly – during those years my reading was improving and I would struggle to read *The Manchester Guardian* instead of *The Mirror*.

I bought a Lambretta motor scooter and sometimes, dressed as a Mod, I would just zoom all over Greater London. But then in leather jacket with the collar turned up I'd be the Wild One, à la Brando; to be really successful as such, though, I'd have to save up to buy a Triumph Thunderbird.

After preening in front of Aunt Lil's front parlour mirror sometime in late 1958, I was about to get my come-uppance. Wearing a new grey mohair overcoat that I'd bought in Genoa on a return trip from Africa and having posed and perfected 'the look' I was away 'up west'. Just as I was nearing the top of the up escalator at Tottenham Court Road, wearing my mohair overcoat like the Italians did, just over my shoulders and with its sash tied casually around my then slim waist, and with recently combed quiff and dark glasses, I could imagine myself to be Fellini or Mastroianni and on my way through Soho to splash in the fountain in Trafalgar Square with Anita Ekberg.

It was at this point, still with the shades on and soon to emerge into a late autumn afternoon, I made up my mind that this day I'd sign no autographs. Arriving at the top of the adjacent down escalator were three blokes in boiler suits carrying a ladder. One caught sight of me and I could almost lip-read what he said to his mates…'Ere Arry look at this twat in his shades!' As we drew level he leaned over to me and said in a loud voice, 'What's it bleedin' sunshiny down there, mate?'

Young man in his hot-rod car, driving like he's mad
In a pair of yellow gloves borrowed from his dad.
He makes it roar so lively just to see his girlfriend smile

But she knows he's only 'putting on the style...'

I didn't know anyone in the Battersea area and as my periods of leave were usually only a couple of weeks at a time, by the time I began to get to know a girl it was time to be off again, any chance of romance nipped in the bud. *'Free and easy, bright and breezy,'* just as the song says, but where exactly were *'all the nice girls to love a sailor'*? They weren't in Battersea, that was for sure, and the problem became acute. I began to long for a girlfriend and really envied those blokes I saw with a girl on their arm.

I signed up and made the return trip to New Zealand on the *Ruahine* and another on the *Rangitoto* in early 1956. On both occasions I took leave and went to visit Mum and Rosie on the sheep station in Martinborough, near Masterton. The place was called Raro-Hiwi, a Maori name meaning 'On the hill', and was of several hundred acres of good grazing and scrubland.

Mr Coleman, then in his late fifties, owned and ran the place on his own. He, like many small farmers, worked long hours at a hard pace and was one of a breed that I had never encountered before. He would often be up and out before first light, taking with him a dog or two. Depending exactly where he was off to on his spread, he would either go on foot or on horseback. Sometimes he'd be gone all day, in which case Mum and Rosie would make him up a packed lunch and had only to cook the evening meal. At other times he would be back as early as nine in the morning and Mum would prepare a breakfast that included steak or chops.

Considering Mum's background she seemed to adjust quite readily to her new lifestyle. The nearest neighbour was two or three miles down the road and although welcoming and friendly, they were busy people and didn't have too much time to spend nattering, which would have suited Mum just fine.

The house was, like many in the country areas of New Zealand, built of wood and on one level only. It was large and had a veranda on three sides. Although comfortable it lacked that certain something that turns a house into a home, and Mum had set-to scrubbing the place from top to bottom, repairing curtains and patching torn upholstery. At a guess, the house might have been built about the turn of the century and it's not too improbable to think that it might have been built by Mr Coleman's father. It had a peaceful feel to it. Its sun-bleached and weathered boards in need of a coat or two of paint, which Mr Coleman no doubt intended to do as soon as he got the time, gave it an air of *'She'll be right, no worries mate':* an attitude that is commonly and refreshingly found in many New Zealanders.

Mr Coleman seemed a shy man. He'd done his bit in the war, had never married and just got on with what he had to do: running the sheep station. He was a tall and stringy individual who seemed tough, not the kind of tough who went around knocking people out but tough and weathered in a self-contained kind of way; stoical and enduring. He didn't talk much, either at the table or after the meal, usually taking himself off to bed at about eight o'clock.

After the war years and the problems that Mum had experienced in her past, this place with its slumbering solitude and its easygoing boss was just the right place for her, almost a convalescent home. At the time, when I was staying there, it didn't occur to me, but since then I have wondered if anything of a romantic nature ever occurred between Mum and Mr Coleman.

Rosie seemed curiously at ease there. Again I didn't think too much about it at the time but it was odd, her acceptance of that way of life. She was seventeen and working as a cross between assistant housekeeper and occasional shepherd, quite different work to the sort of jobs that she would have found back home in London. It had been over two years since Dad's death and Rosie seemed simple and always smiling in rather an inane sort of way. I was eighteen and just saw her as a contented kid. Later, however, I came to the conclusion that some essential clock within her had stopped ticking since my father's death. Mum being such a dominant 'no-nonsense' woman might have become too possessive or controlling toward Rosie for her to have left home and found her own independence. These opinions never occurred at the time of course, and being immature and greedy for my own freedom made me too selfish to consider Rosie's future. Even as she got older I never thought of her as Rose but always Rosie.

As I waved goodbye to them from the bus at Masterton, their figures beside the dusty road seemed to shrink as the bus gathered speed. I didn't know then that I wouldn't be seeing them again for nearly three years, and when I did that our lives would have taken quite a twist.

By now, in the summer of 1956, I had spent two or three periods of leave back in London and had began to make visits back to Kingsbury and Belvedere Way, where the Council had housed us after the war, hoping to pick up again with the old gang from the street and from Claremont Secondary Modern School. John Lewis had followed the example of Vic and me and had joined up. When I called on him he was away with the Orient Line to Kobe and Yokohama, in Japan: somewhere I never got to. I left my address with his mum and dad but it was quite a while before I saw him again as when he was home I was away again. I found the same problem in trying to contact Vic. His parents were so very welcoming, though, and told me there was always a bed in their home for me should I ever need one.

Derek Westwood, another boyhood friend whom I never got to see, had managed deferment from National Service because of an apprenticeship he was doing and was involved in great things in his leisure time. I learnt from his dad that he had got into the music scene, managing musicians and arranging bookings for them in various clubs. It was at about that time - I learnt many years later - that he met and married Vivienne, who went on to become known as Vivienne Westwood. With the proceeds Derek made from his entrepreneurial skills he would put himself through flying school, eventually becoming a pilot for BOAC.

David Marsh had been conscripted and was now in the RAF, probably improvising on the *Dambusters* theme on his violin. Kevin Brennan, once my closest mate, had taken off. The Ellingfords made me welcome whenever I called and there was always a cup of tea, but their children weren't around either. Steven had married Barbara, the girl next door, and one day in the future they too would emigrate to New Zealand.

Everyone seemed to have taken off and there was no sign of Uncle Snowy. The street appeared smaller and somehow more vulnerable. There was a new, younger gang in the street playing cricket, and I felt a stranger, wraith-like and lost. So much change had happened in the past eighteen months that I guess I was attempting to regain a foothold on what could be termed normality. Change, and more change; there was to be plenty more of it ahead for me, and not all of it pleasant.

A Guest of General Franco

He wasn't a tall man, perhaps about my height, but he was built like a bull. A Spanish bull, fiery and hostile. He had rattled off something in rapid Spanish to the other man in the room, who had then gone to a cupboard and taken from it a large stick which was now in the big bull's right fist. He was repeatedly smacking it lightly into his left palm as he spoke to me, his eyes glittering dangerously beneath thick and wiry brows. '¡En Ingleterra, No! ¡Per aqui, Si!' (In England, No!, but here, Yes!)

There were three of us in the brightly-lit room, two policemen in plain clothes and me. The room was of moderate size and white-washed. It contained a table, three chairs and a cupboard. There were no windows but a grill set high in one of the walls may have admitted daylight or even sunshine at certain times of the day, although I had no way of knowing. I had been brought to this room from a communal cell along the passageway where I had been held for several hours, how many exactly I didn't know as I had lost track of the time. If I had to make a guess I'd say it was now about four in the morning. I had drifted in and out of sleep throughout a restless night spent sitting on the floor of the communal cell, my back against the wall. There had been a lot of coming and going since we'd arrived and it had become fairly crowded.

At about midnight there had been about eight of us in there, all Spanish except for me. One bloke had been carried in unconscious, his face in a real mess and blood all over the front of his shirt. The acoustics of the place seemed to magnify even the smallest of sounds; keys jangled, locks turned, doors slammed, footsteps reverberated and from time to time, during the long night, harsh and angry voices had echoed along the corridor followed by occasional grunts and cries. At one point I had been woken from a catnap by the sound of male laughter and a woman protesting in shrieks and cries. She had sounded in pain.

Lawson and I had been frog-marched in handcuffs along a busy street at about six o'clock the previous evening. The arrest seemed unbelievable, all the more so because only moments before the shopkeeper had been so accommodating, smiling at us from behind the counter of his jewellery shop as he explained in good English why this gem was so much more valuable than that, the quality of a particular stone and the setting. Suddenly the police were there and the shopkeeper, not smiling now but aggressive and shrill of voice, was speaking rapidly, his arms and shoulders in motion, his hands pointing to trays of rings and watches and then at us. We'd been at it of course, trying to nick whatever we could, but I began to wonder just how sane Lawson was when he denied totally what we'd been doing. We'd been caught bang-to-rights and I knew that Lawson had the goods on him. But no! He was shaking his head vigorously and looking totally amazed that anyone should even begin to think that we could do such a thing.

'Theese man say you tak heesmmm hewellery. Si?' said one of the policemen, addressing us in what I thought were very reasonable tones. Lawson continued to look shocked.

'Theese man say you gheeve them to heem again back and he forget and we all... go home, yes?' continued the cop. What a very good idea, I thought with relief, ready to agree to such a reasonable proposal and even to promise with my hand on my heart never ever to do such a thing again.

Lawson was made of sterner stuff however, and looking stolid began a sort of, 'How-dare-you-even-think-we-could-stoop-to-such-a- thing' speech, which although very good, to give him his due, was not good enough. The shopkeeper then got even more excited over our denial and now - despite me smiling at him - purple of hue in the face he was seriously beginning to approach meltdown. There had followed a lot of rapid and loud Spanish back and forth between the police, the shopkeeper and his wife, who had now joined us, and even one or two of the customers in the shop seemed to be putting in their two pesetas' worth. It resulted in us having to empty our pockets onto the counter, but whatever it was that had been nicked just wasn't among the contents that lay there. Perhaps Lawson had perfected sleight of hand? I didn't know him that well and he was proving to be full of surprises. Maybe he was a member of the Magic Circle or in fact had swallowed whatever it was that was apparently missing.

Our M.O., Modus Operandi (I think that's the term) was as follows; we would enter a shop and I would keep the owner or assistant busy, perhaps asking to see something and Lawson would case the joint ready to exercise nimble fingers if the opportunity arose. It had worked on several occasions and we'd successfully fenced a trinket or two through a bootblack who worked in the market, making enough pesetas to allow us a decent meal and a few drinks. All that, however, was now history and what was the present – ever so present – was this big Mussolini look-a-like, waving a big stick and looking annoyed over my refusal to co-operate.

What I was refusing to do was to sign a typed confession which stated that I, Peter Joseph Troy, had collaborated with one David Lawson, to steal an amount of jewellery from one Miguel Da-Costa. Well I think that's what it said. They'd spelt our names right but the rest was all in Spanish so I couldn't be sure. If I signed something that I didn't fully understand I might be signing a confession to overthrow the state. At eighteen I wasn't too clued up on world affairs but I did know the Spanish had a different system of government, like a gang of one. And hadn't it been the Spanish who had conducted the Inquisition?

The big fellow in front of me, now holding a big stick and looking as if his patience was about to expire, might have been a descendant of Torquemada, or whoever it was who was responsible. Okay, maybe I'm sounding cocky now about my situation then, but I really was scared and didn't know what to do. My request to see someone from the Consul's office had been denied and I hadn't seen anything of Lawson since we'd been brought in and strip-searched, a search that had revealed nothing of immediate interest to the authorities. On our frog-march through the town, Lawson had mumbled to me not to admit or sign anything but to 'front it out', and with hindsight that might have been the most important advice ever given to me. Thanks for that, Lawson, wherever you are. If you read this get in touch and I'll put you in my will.

After the search we had been separated and my imagination, being what it was, compelled me to believe that every time during the night that I heard a cry it was Lawson being put to hot irons.

The angry bloke with the big stick hadn't used it and was allowing his fellow cop, who might have said something regarding the British Consul, to take it and put it back in the cupboard. I didn't say anything or give him one of my customary smiles or even establish eye contact. Despite my prudence, I wasn't going to get off completely scot free from this encounter. The stick might have gone but his anger was still present and he was beginning to look even more irritated and began shouting in my face, releasing evidence of a meal taken earlier which had been heavily spiced with garlic. He needed to assert himself physically, that much was certain, and banging his large fist down on the table several times didn't seem to be helping him.

At the end of his tether, he began to smack me about the head and face with heavy blows of his open hand. Cuffing, backhanding and shouting words and spittle at me, he followed me about the room whilst I backed away and tried to escape. With my hands up trying to protect my head and my body wide open he delivered his 'coup de grace'. With a full fist he hit me very hard in the kidneys. It drove all the air from my lungs and choking I fell to the floor, trying to vomit the pain away but nothing would come. Had he started in with his boots then I'm convinced it would have been all over for me. I would have expired on the spot. But no, that was it, thank God! I wasn't pressured again to sign anything and when I could stand I was allowed to slink back, bent double, to the communal cell.

***

I had joined the P & O Liner, the S.S. *Iberia*, as a utility steward in Southampton on July 7th, 1956, and taken anything that would put me onto an adult rating's pay. So I found myself put to work in the plate-house operating the dish-washing machines. It was there I had met Dave Lawson, a tall, clean-cut fellow with a public school background. In appearance he was similar to a young Roger Bannister with straw coloured hair which hung lank over one eye, and it wasn't too difficult to imagine him in a Harrow boater or a Henley blazer. Considering our different backgrounds it now seems strange how well we clicked. I found him interesting, amusing and witty and because we worked together and our time off coincided we went ashore together. The ship had put in at Gibraltar and then, once into the Med, had hugged the Algerian coast until we arrived at Malta, where Lawson and I had explored that part of Valletta known as 'The Gut', an area mainly composed of bars, dives and brothels. It was well known and frequented by the Royal Navy and seamen over many years. It was there in a bar and over a bottle of the local brew known as Screech (about two bob a pint) that we first talked wildly of jumping ship and just doing a summer- runner through Europe. We didn't do it there and then but the idea had been planted and in the warm, moist atmosphere of the plate-house it began to germinate.

From Malta the ship sailed northeast and up through the straits of Messina. It was just beyond there that I saw a sight that has remained with me since. If, from the straits, you then set a course northwest for Naples you have to sail close to Stromboli, an active volcanic island in the Tyrrhenian Sea. As the ship approached the island at dusk we saw directly above the mouth of the volcano a cloud that reflected on its underside, in an orange glow, all the seething activity that was taking place deep inside the scalding pit. The bridge telegraph sounded and our engine speed began to drop as it became apparent that the skipper was going to circle the island, giving all those on board an opportunity to observe this phenomenon.

As we circled the sky grew darker and night began to fall, which increased the glow to the base of the cloud that was changing from orange through red to crimson, searching and revealing all the hues in that part of the spectrum to display before us. Once we were to the west of Stromboli we could see, spilling from the volcano's lip, great droplets of molten red lava that rolled down its side and fell into the sea where they began to spit and hiss midst clouds of steam. It was the most amazing sight and, having witnessed it, I could readily understand the awe that it and similar sights must have inspired in primitive man, or maybe in Odysseus and other early wanderers.

The ship didn't stop at Naples but continued northwest along the Italian coast until we arrived at Civitavecchia, from where many of the passengers took an excursion to Rome. For some reason there was no shore leave for crew so when the ship arrived in Palma, Majorca a couple of days later, and when lunch was over and Lawson and I had finished in the plate-house, we couldn't wait to get ashore.

By the time we had finished - all plates washed and machines turned off - and had showered and changed and got into the liberty boat with about a dozen sleepy passengers, the clock was pushing three. Neither of us had been to Palma before so when we stepped out onto the hot marina we just followed our feet. They led us away from the water and along narrow cobbled streets dappled in bright sunshine and cool shadow. We climbed steps and wound our way upward through alleyways and archways that were hushed and deserted. Shuttered windows and curtained doors concealed dark and spicy secrets as houses and shops slumbered peacefully beneath lines of washing that hung starched and dry through the hot afternoon. As we trespassed through, a large Dalmatian bitch lay sprawled in shade. She yawned and blinked at us, then dropped back into her siesta.

Shore leave was due to expire at six o'clock for departure at seven but we still had time for a decent drink as the shadows began to lengthen, and we entered a small bar that had just opened. Sitting in a shady patio that looked out over the bay and the *Iberia* at anchor, we found Cognac at the equivalent of sixpence a large tot almost too good to be true. What became even more of an attraction were the two young women who entered through the small gateway covered with bougainvillea and seated themselves nearby. The one who wore an orange dress and a straw hat ordered from the waiter, revealing they were both English. They were in animated conversation and seemed to be having a simply marvellous time, the ice tinkling in their drinks as they prattled on.

'Mummy thought he was an absolute scream, a real hoot. But Daddy! Well you know Daddy...' They were definitely playing to the gallery where Lawson and I were sitting.

'I say!' called Lawson, full of confidence. 'Would you mind terribly if my chum and I joined you both?'

'Well...' replied the straw hat, looking coy and aware that we had not been formally introduced.

I hadn't seen this side of Lawson before, the ladies man. He began to ooze charm when we were settled at their table, a charm to which both women proved highly susceptible. Responding warmly to his wit they chortled and listened to him, their eyes shining, and with lips moist and slightly apart they devoured his subtle flattery. Feeling thick and wooden when Lawson introduced us both, I decided to play the strong silent type: still waters run deep. The straw hat was Cynthia and my one with the glasses, if it ever came to that, was Muriel. When Lawson suggested drinks all round I took the cue and went off into the bar in search of a waiter.

We, Lawson and I, were 'Doing Europe' I learned after I got back to the table. The drinks arrived shortly and I settled the bill, leaving on the tray a generous and hopefully impressive tip. Had we come this far on the liner in the bay? Yes, that's right, and we were researching Moorish influences on Western architecture. The women seemed impressed and so was I. Lawson talked on in an entertaining way, witty and urbane, and I tried to keep up and 'not let the side down, old man' when they drew me into their conversation.

Two liberty launches chugged their way through the water below us, trailing a white wake against the intense blue of the bay, ferrying passengers back from the marina to the platform at the base of the gangway. A gull hovered. The late afternoon sun lay warm on my back as Lawson waffled on; its steady amber glow slanted, falling across the table and lit the bare, brown arms of Cynthia's friend, Muriel. Her expensive watch, small and golden, sparkled and revealed the time: twenty to six. Lawson stood. We were both going to be late back, and I stood as well.

'No rush, Troy old man. I'll order another bottle.' And off went Lawson, leaving me to hold the fort. Awkwardly I tried to do so, but what to say? I racked my brains but then Muriel took the initiative and asked about our research, were we being funded? I began to answer, my brain in over-drive, but as I did so the *Iberia* let forth a blast on her siren that echoed about the bay, calling the last passengers and crew to join her. Just then Lawson arrived back smiling, with a bottle of chilled white wine and four fresh glasses.

Whether we were 'rebels without a cause' I'm not certain. The film had hit the screen the year before so perhaps you could say we were playing our own form of 'chicken', seeing which of us would bolt and run first. What in the name of Christ were we doing or hoping to achieve? Who was all such bravado for? There was no hint of such a question then for us, but the answer has to be that the bravado was for ourselves, each other. It wasn't for the women, they weren't even aware of the game we were playing. Staying cool was important. The last liberty boat came and went, but it still wasn't too late. We only had to say goodbye to the women, walk on down to the agents, the harbour master or even the chandlers and a way could have been found to get us back on board. We'd have been in trouble, sure, up on the bridge before the skipper for a logging and to lose a day's pay but no - it was important to play the game out.

Determined to call Lawson's bluff I excused myself from the table as the ship let off another blast. He was regaling the women with a story about his schooldays at Charterhouse or Rugby or wherever, as I went off in search of another bottle. All a bit 'squiffy', we topped up our glasses all round. It was ten to seven and Lawson showed no concern at all.

'Oh look! She's getting up steam,' said Cynthia and pointed out into the bay. Another blast and the ship, our ship, had swung about ready to depart. We all stood and toasted her as she sailed away, watching her until she rounded the headland and was gone. The ship had gone and all our possessions with it. By seven-thirty so had the women, gone to join their families for dinner. Lawson and I reported and explained our predicament to the harbour master, who in turn phoned the agents.

At half past eight we were eating paella and had been secured a bed for the night in a modest but comfortable pension. The days that followed included a round of trips to the agent's offices where telegrams were dispatched and received back and forth to Leadenhall Street, London. Arrangements were made for us to join the *Chusan*, another of the company's vessels, due to arrive in about a week's time. Our accommodation, inclusive of meals, was arranged, but there would be no advancement of wages: we were in disgrace. And we had almost no money left. We shouldn't have turned to petty crime, of course, but we did.

By the time that the *Chusan* arrived, we were both under lock and key. My ribs were still hurting from the punch I'd received and my pee was pink. Not wanting to worry Mum and Rosie and proceeding on the basis that no news is good news, I withheld their address in New Zealand and hoped that Uncle Dick would do the same.

```
                                    Telephone Avenue 8000
                                    Telegrams Peninsular London Telex
   P & O                            Cables Peninsular London
                                    Telex No 8624
       Peninsular and Oriental Steam Navigation Company

                  Superintendent Purser
Please address reply to The Managing Director    122 LEADENHALL STREET LONDON EC3

Mrs. Troy,
5, Beaufoy Road,
Battersea,                          20th August, 1956
London, S.W.11.

Dear Madam,
           I wish to inform you that I have been advised by the
Company's Agents at Palma that your son Peter Joseph Troy
failed to rejoin the "IBERIA" at that port.  Arrangements were
made for him to be repatriated to London in the "CHUSAN", but I
have since learned that he has been involved in a police case
ashore and is being detained.

                    Yours faithfully,

                    SUPERINTENDENT PURSER
                         (R.H.Hayward)
```

On the same morning that I had received my smacking, but much later at about eleven o'clock, I was taken in handcuffs to a busy office in the Palace of Justice where Lawson was waiting, also in handcuffs and with a puffy face and split lip. We nodded at each other but didn't attempt to talk and were soon joined by a man who turned out to be on the Consular staff. He was Spanish but explained to us in very good English that we were to be officially charged with theft even though there was little evidence at present. He also explained to us that our trial might take some time as the courts were very busy. Her Majesty's Consul would try to do everything to hurry things up and would be in touch with us on a regular basis. Meanwhile was there anything that we needed: toothbrush, soap, etc.? Anything that was provided we would, of course, have to sign and eventually pay for.

***

'*Cuchara*,' said the prisoner, holding up his spoon. '*Cuchara*,' I repeated. I was learning Spanish and we'd been in the Prision Provinciale for the past week. I of course really had no idea what to expect but to be honest it wasn't that bad. Lawson and I shared a cell with two other prisoners and weren't banged up during the day but allowed to roam about. It was a large and very old building that at one time had been a monastery for Capuchin monks.

There was a large central courtyard with passages off that led to cells, crude latrines, showers and sinks. On the floor above there were more cells and a balcony overlooking the courtyard. The guards were a mixed bunch and some it was wise to be wary of and show respect to. Lawson and I were regarded with a certain amount of curiosity as we were the only Brits in the place. The other prisoners, all of whom were Spanish and appeared resigned to their sentences, were well behaved and polite but kept us at a discreet distance, not asking too many questions or volunteering much in the way of information.

There was no special uniform for prisoners and many of the inmates were, like us, still wearing the clothes they had been wearing when arrested. In many cases these clothes had over time become little more than patched and patched again rags which when washed had to be treated with great care. Each morning at about eight o'clock the prisoners formed an orderly queue and Lawson and I soon learned to be in it or go hungry. We had been issued a wooden bowl and a *cuchara*, and as we got to the head of the queue we were given a small loaf of bread. Because we did not have a mug or cup, our ladle-full of warm milk was poured into our bowl. Following the example of most of the other prisoners we sat or squatted on the cobblestones in the courtyard, our backs resting against a wall. A common practice was to tear off about a third of your loaf, putting what was left into your shirt front, and then breaking the third into pieces to put it into the milk, just like Mum had often done for Rosie and me when we'd been kids. You had to be sure to keep a close eye on what was left of your loaf because if you put it down for a moment it had a habit of vanishing. If it did then you had to wait until next morning before you got another one. At about midday and then at about six in the evening we formed queues and were fed again. Lunch and dinner were usually the same fare and nearly always consisted of fish or goat stew.

In the corner of the courtyard each afternoon at about four-thirty a small queue formed. A shutter was removed and the prison shop opened for business. Those who could afford to bought bread, olive oil, fresh vegetables and fruit. Tinned goods were also available and perhaps more importantly so was tobacco. Items could also be ordered. So who had money? The answer to that were those who worked. Although no-one in the prison was forced to, the prisoners were encouraged to work. Materials were provided for the manufacture of woven goods: baskets, bags, mats, hats and other items which when completed were sold through the gift shops of Palma. The wages, although low, were enough to make the difference between a bland diet of only bread and stew and something more enjoyable such as a salad, a tin of sardines or even a peach. A man's attitude was of course noticed and a worker was more likely to receive a more sympathetic hearing when, or if, he came up before the parole board.

The first week was something of a novelty despite our loss of liberty. Lawson and I were still playing bravado but I have to say that, despite what happened later, he was an interesting buddy to be in the nick with. For a start he was the only other English speaking bloke in there, so we tended to have long conversations on all manner of subjects, and I was never bored by him. Annoyed and irritated at times, but never bored. He taught me to play chess and that in itself was a tremendous resource to have in that place and at that time.

It happened at lunchtime just as we were standing in the queue. One of the prisoners ahead of me snapped and went berserk. Having just received his helping of stew, he then ran forward, throwing the bowl and its contents at one of the guards. A whistle blew and in moments the courtyard was full of uniformed guards, their truncheons drawn. It was clear that such things had happened before as all the prisoners ran to the far wall and stood in line facing it. I was a bit slow and received a heavy truncheon blow to my elbow before I got to the wall. I would be as quick as the others if it happened again, I resolved. Facing the wall and rubbing my bruised elbow I couldn't see what was going on behind me as I dare not turn my head, but my ears were telling me a lot. The prisoner was still shouting and screaming but the guards had him cornered and sounded as if they were laying into him with their truncheons. The sound of hard wood on flesh and bone is distinctive and once heard is not easily forgotten. With each blow his cries became initially louder, but then fainter until only a whimpering could be heard as they took their time targeting their blows with greater accuracy; and then even his whimper was cut off abruptly with a wet, whopping, crunching sound as wood struck teeth and jaw.

A silence descended instantly all about, broken only by the sound of someone along the line vomiting up his guts. I became aware that all the muscles in my body had gone into spasm and my teeth were gritted. I was hunched over with my eyes shut tight and my arms crossed. Each hand gripping as tightly as I could an elbow, I tried to make myself as small as possible. I was engulfed in a mixture of fear, hatred and outrage so intense that at the time I couldn't recognize my emotions for what they were. No-one moved. I don't know what the man was inside for but maybe the prospect of a very long sentence stretching before him into middle age had seemed unbearable and might well have tipped his mind and been the reason he'd gone berserk.

The weeks had clocked up their first month and we were now into mid September, my nineteenth birthday had come and gone and if I remembered it at the time then I don't recall.

'Psst!' The place is buzzing, rumours are going round.

'A new man is in, he came in late last night, his arm in a sling.'

'He's English and he's the skipper off an M.T.B. now under police guard in Palma.'

'His leg, it's broken and he's on crutches.'

'He's not English but American and he's not the skipper only the mate.'

'No, no he's not in yet, he's still in the hospital and it's touch and go he's so full of bullet holes.'

'No, no, Ramon told me and he knows, the man is Portuguese but speaks American with an English accent and there is no boat.'

'No, you're both wrong. He's French.'

'It's Errol Flynn.' (His yacht *Zaca* was moored in Palma at the time).

The rumours became more absurd by the hour until there were rumours about the rumours and 'Guess who said what?'

We weren't to see him for almost a week but then he appeared one morning, standing in the line ahead of me, waiting for his bread and milk. Slightly stooped and with rounded shoulders, his tall figure looked as if for many years he had lived in a confined space. Draped about his frame was an old leather flying jacket, well-worn and stained across its back with paint or more likely red-lead. It wasn't until he'd received his loaf and bowl of milk and had turned about looking for somewhere to squat that I saw that his right arm was in a sling. He was a hollow looking individual, gaunt and drawn of features with several days' growth upon his jowls. Although curiosity about him was intense, the protocol to allow him his space and time was paramount so no-one approached him on that first day or indeed the next. If we ever knew his real name whatever it was is now long forgotten, but Lawson and I nicknamed him Captain Flag. I worked with him a week or two later, white-washing a wall together and without too much prying into his business, I learnt a little of his circumstances, more of which later.

Lawson and I were getting bored with the food. It was nourishing enough but cool stew everyday was getting us down. Something had to be done. The man from the Consul's office had been to see us twice, and on each occasion we had badgered him on the chances of bail, but the authorities would not allow it, or so he had told us. I knew that I had wages left on the *Iberia* and had asked if they could not be made available to me. The man had said he would try to arrange for their transfer and would let us know next time he came. Time was dragging by and we seemed to be no nearer to a date for a trial. At times I thought that if they served me stew again I would hurl it in someone's face, but the memory of what had happened to the poor devil that had done just that remained indelibly etched in my brain. Just what had been his fate after they'd dragged his unconscious body away? The question wouldn't go away. The only response I could get if I carefully asked around was a forefinger to the lips (Sshh, don't ask) and a mime that involved an imaginary large stick.

During the past couple of weeks one of the prisoners, Phillipe, had on several occasions admired my shirt. Although most of the buttons had gone, it still washed up almost like new. It was a Rael-Brook, drip-dry with French cuffs and a cutaway collar, in fact the same shirt that we'd clad Gallagher in a lifetime ago. After it was washed and dried, taken off its hanger and slipped on, it provided one of the few pleasures that were still available to me. It was a tangible reminder of the shop in Oxford Street where I'd bought it and of the young woman shop assistant with whom I'd flirted at the time. Furthermore it reinforced an image that I held of myself. The cinema often portrayed its heroes in a white shirt – the Prisoner of Zenda, the Count of Monte Christo, Dartagnan: imprisoned fictional heroes that I romantically identified with. Daft, I know, but then I was only just nineteen and had always been a dreamer. Perhaps Phillipe secretly saw himself as a musketeer, too, as he requested first refusal if I ever thought of selling the shirt. My mind turned the idea over as I lay on my straw mattress one night, and what it really came down to was my image for an orange, and perhaps another loaf and some tomatoes, maybe some oil and sardines, and even some sugar. The following morning I went to look for Phillipe.

The deal, after much haggling and trying on, was this. For forty pesetas (about four shillings) he would swap his shirt, a worn and faded blue article without a collar, for mine. We shook hands on the deal which was a sort of 'exchange of contracts'. At about four o'clock, after both shirts had been washed and dried (I could almost taste that orange), we completed. Before I got in the queue for the shop, Phillipe put in a bid for my trousers. But some things are not negotiable.

***

Something was wrong, but I didn't know what. It wasn't that the place was quiet – it was never noisy – but a different sort of quietness seemed to prevail. The men's faces looked grim, grimmer than usual, and I felt uncomfortable. What was going on? Then later, after the evening meal, about an hour before bang-up and as I was coming out from the wash-house with a damp towel about me I knew. Coming toward me slowly two men were helping a third to walk. He was between them hobbling, being half carried. The effort involved seemed considerable. I stood to one side to give them access and then looked closer. The man in the middle was the man who had gone berserk weeks earlier in the yard. It was difficult to recognize him; he looked as if he had been involved in a car accident or worse. The red weals and dried blood across his pale and battered face stood out starkly. His eyes were totally empty, unfocussed and staring, an empty shell; a husk of a head without any teeth. The stench as they passed was nauseating and one of the men helping was sobbing loudly.

For the next two days our freedom to wander about was severely curtailed. An hour after each meal we were banged up in our cells and the mood of the prisoners seemed truculent and resentful. The guards seemed nervous and more vigilant as if they feared a backlash of anger over the incident. Lawson told me that he'd heard that the broken man had received a thrashing every night since being taken and put into solitary. He'd also learnt that *bastinado* had been used on him, a form of torture that involves thrashing the soles of the feet with a steel rod. I found that hard to believe at the time. Torture being used to extract a confession or reveal information: it's inhumane to be sure, but at least there's a medieval logic to it. What I had difficulty in accepting was torture being used purely as a means of punishment.

Had I known at the time quite who Franco was I would have been afraid, very afraid. Spain then was a totalitarian state and its leader, General Francisco Franco, was the last one of three brutal dictators who came to power in Europe between the wars. His friends had been Hitler and Mussolini and they had been dealt with. Franco lived on, his regime built on terror, torture and mass murder. Thank God Lawson and I were in for nothing more than alleged theft. Had we been suspected of being members of an anarchist organization or of holding communist sympathies then we might have been subject to the same fate as others so suspected, and that would have been to die a horrible death in one of his torture chambers. Was there ever a better time to have been politically naïve?

Peter Joseph Troy

Out

On the 26th of September we were released on bail. As simple as that! We'd awoken that morning and started the same routine, not knowing that the man from the Consul's office would come in at about ten o'clock with a paper allowing our release. We'd been arrested seven weeks earlier and now we were out. Out again midst the bustle of people and traffic, it seemed so noisy. That walk from the prison to the Consul's office was the most marvellous walk ever. There was immediacy about everything - a heightened awareness. The midday sun, so bright, so hot, lit the old buildings in strong contrasting tones. We passed the Plaza Mayor where people sat out in the open air savouring their drinks, their *ensaimadas*: their freedom. Women! I hadn't seen one since my arrest so I devoured the sight of them, their shape, the way they moved, their voices, their colourful dresses. They and everything seemed to be so alive. Cars and scooters buzzed about, hooting and honking; their drivers and riders in shirt sleeves looked so free, free to go wherever they wanted. Even the fumes from traffic exhaust had the whiff of freedom. We were free, too. I was exultant.

At the Consul's office we were brought up to date with our situation. We had been granted bail on my surety. The wages that I'd earned aboard the *Iberia* had been telegraphed from London, a total of £21-15-9. Bail stood at five hundred pesetas each (about five pounds). The balance would be used to find accommodation and full pension for us until our trial. A date had yet to be set for that and probably would not take place for a few weeks. Lawson had very little wages left in the ship and the assumption was made that I would stand for him, too. Under the circumstances their assumption was correct. I was so pleased to be out that I think I would have agreed to marry him had it been a condition for our release. Lawson was, of course, coolly grateful and promised to repay me as soon as we got back to England. After signing various papers, their translations being made available to us, we were then walked around to the Pension Soller in the Calle Vallori where we registered. I had not written to Mum and Rosie, hoping they would assume no news is good news. I had however dropped a line to Uncle Dick to put his mind at rest, and requested he keep any worrisome news from Mum in New Zealand.

Our trial, we learnt within a day or two, was to take place in late October, nearly a month away. How were we to manage till then? What if we were found guilty, what term of imprisonment lay before us and where would we serve it? I tried not to show it, of course (tried again not to let the side down, old man), but had never been so full of confused feelings and worries: relieved to be out, worried about the possible outcome of the trial and dismayed to find that everything was taking so long.

For the first week or so to be at liberty was enough: the three good meals a day, a room to myself a bonus. We made friends with Andre, the tall waiter at the Pension Soller. He could have passed for a guardsman with his bushy moustache and smart appearance. He loaned Lawson a shirt and supplied us both with bait and fishing lines with which we tried our luck at various places around the bay and the port. We saw Captain Flag's boat, the *Amanda Mary*, tied up at the end of a jetty, peppered with bullet holes, an armed guard patrolling her deck. We encountered English and American tourists and found that by dreaming up plausible stories for our circumstances (but not admitting our guilt) they often bought us drinks and sometimes gave us a hand-out. The time slipped by; first a week, then another. The hot autumn days began to give way to cool evenings and cooler nights. The billboards were full of the news of Suez. Budapest too was becoming an issue as the Soviet tanks rolled in. World events were spiralling and our future looked uncertain.

'But what if we're found guilty, what happens then?' I tried to keep the note of panic out of my voice. Lawson and I were sitting on the dock, with our baited lines patiently awaiting a tug.

'Could be a penal colony, with maybe five years hard,' muttered Lawson.

'What d'you reckon it is here,' I queried, trying to stay cool, covering up my increasing concern, 'quarries or mailbags?'

'Haven't the foggiest, old man,' muttered Lawson in that unconcerned, upper class way that he always seemed to have about him. I restrained an impulse to violently shove him into the dock (the fish might be rising soon to take the bait, but I wasn't taking Lawson's). The air was warm and the current pop song was reaching us on the breeze from someone's transistor radio... *'Migusta mi novia. Porque? Muchas Cosa's.'* I forced myself to hum along with it, waiting for a tug, the water beneath me unfathomable, just like Lawson.

***

'If you wasn't on a goddamned island you could try for the border.' With nicotined fingers Digroce peels a strand of tobacco from his tongue, and then continues. 'You could try for France maybe, or better still Gibraltar, that's British.' Behind the clink of cocktails and hum of happy talk, the tantalizing smells of paella and fish grilling are playing havoc with my appetite. I haven't eaten since noon and I'm starving. Late sunlight streams across the white tablecloth, a clock strikes eight and I wonder if I'm going to make it as I won't be eating until after nine back at the Pension Soller.

Digroce (rhymes with Josie) is from 'Noo Yark City, back in the old U S of A'. His brother, so he'd told me earlier, was looking after the liquor store on Long Island whilst he and Myrtle take their first real holiday in 'twenny' years.

'Yes sir, that's us out there.' From within a blue wreath of cigar smoke he nods at the American cruise liner anchored out in the bay. 'And a damn fine ship she is, too – ain't that right, Honey?' From our perspective the vessel, bathed in the Mediterranean evening light and with its decks and masts all lit with what appear to be fairy lights, seems an even more idealised version of itself. Despite my tramp-like appearance the three of us have fallen into easy conversation in this pavement cafe that looks out over the bay in Palma.

Digroce is an old and scrawny guy of maybe forty-five or so. He has a hawkish nose and a balding head and if it wasn't for the blue seersucker suit, the cigar clamped in the corner of his mouth and the silver-rimmed glasses there'd be something biblical, almost Samaritan-like, about him. We sit sipping pale sherry and whether it's the sight of the sun descending over the bay, or my desire to confide in someone that loosens my inner reserve I can't say.

Something's shifted, has given me permission to drop all the subterfuge that I normally employ when talking to strangers and I just open up. I hear myself gabbing away twenty to the dozen, telling both Digroce and Myrtle everything. Is it a cry for help, a simple confession or just a telling of the way things are? They both sit relaxed, yet attentive as I spill the beans, telling them of my jumping ship with Lawson back in July. I tell them of the jewellers and the police and the charges brought against us. Digroce looks as if he's a man who has tasted life so I don't go into the details of the prison. I don't need to for it's pure therapy just being able to talk to people who are prepared to listen in a non-judgmental way. He nods occasionally as I rattle away whilst Myrtle looks calmly on. Although I feel unburdened and grateful to them for listening to me it really doesn't alter a damn thing. Bail is a million times better than jail but it's still a far cry from freedom. Right now I'd swap my youth for Digroce's hawk nose and balding head, his soft plump wife, his liberty.

On my way back to the Pension Soller through the Arab quarter, I weave my way in and out of a strolling cosmopolitan crowd: a babble of voices, German, French, English and others mingling through a mixture of peculiar smells. There's a distinctive whiff of Turkish tobacco, fragrant scent, hot oil and after shave. I duck down cobbled steps, cut through dark alleyways and into small plazas where children play, dogs bark, lamps burn and laundry hangs. I pass bootblacks and newsstands from which galleries of grim international faces peer out from the front covers of papers and magazines: photos of Eden, Nasser and John Foster Dulles, all in dispute over Suez. If this isn't enough there's also Khrushchev's baby-face adding weight to the rumours of Russian tanks getting ready to roll into Budapest.

Captain Flag had been right in his assessment; the world is up in arms. 'What times to go gun-running,' he'd sighed in broken English weeks earlier as we'd worked together, whitewashing walls in the prison compound. The Captain had been carrying a shipment of small arms from Marseilles to Oran when his boat had been challenged in moonlight off the Minorca coast. He'd tried to make a run for it but the Spanish Customs and Excise had opened fire, riddling his boat full of holes. It was from him I learned that there existed small companies of smugglers, one of which he worked for. To be able to speak English was important and the pay was high, he told me.

'You want - I could see you right man for work. Si? You not have wife or kiddie, you get rich, plenty monies, plenty women yes.'

It sounded exciting to me, and might one day look good on my CV. I could impress future mates, women and my uncle Jim. Oh Yes! I was off on another Walter Mitty journey. (I did warn you I was a poser.) I'd be deeply tanned, grow a moustache, wear a white shirt with French cuffs, might even wear a red bandana around my head, perhaps a small scar just above my right eyebrow... Oh yes!

'But your boat, it's full of bullet holes. Did anyone get hurt?' I asked.

'Si, si sure he more than hurt.'

'Who got hurt?'

'Carlo – he dead.'

...Sod that! I forgot all about red bandanas.

***

When I get back to the Pension Soller I go straight into the dining room and sit at our allotted table. Lawson is there already, tearing into a bread roll whilst Andre, the waiter, ladles fish soup from a tureen into his plate. It smells delicious. Lawson is, of course, always as hungry as I am, so we're never late for our meals.

'Okay, old man,' he manages to mutter in that absent way he has about him. We seldom chat at all now, as there is nothing new to say. I don't mention my meeting with the Digroces, and certainly nothing about the plan that has begun to infect my brain. It's easy to be secretive because of the resentments that have developed between the two of us. Resentment is natural, I suppose, between two people who have been involuntarily yoked together for too long. We both bolt down our supper and I go to my room early and flake out on the bed. I need to be on my own to think things through. It's that remark of Digroce's about being on an island and talk of crossing borders that has given my brain something to feed on. Do I really want Lawson with me if I try anything? It's his 'old man this' and 'old man that' which has, over the past few months, seriously begun to get on my tit.

Digroce's words concerning the French border, my own reflections, and then my planning and plotting have given me a restless night. I've considered all the angles and have decided to let Lawson in on the plan. He was all attention, listening to what I had to say. We were in his room and it was before breakfast. I'd made up my mind to try it on my own if he decided against the idea. The way I saw it, we had little to lose, and maybe several years of freedom to gain. I could tell it was a great scheme by the way Lawson was wearing his thinking cap (in decent clothes he could have passed for Raffles).

'So she sails at four today. That means last launch at, what, two, three o'clock?' He was considering it.

'Yeah, but we don't want the last one, do we?' I said. 'The security will be stricter then, we want an earlier one, about midday.'

We kept well back, sitting on the sea-wall watching the liberty boat making repeated trips back and forth to the liner's launch platform at the bottom of its companionway. It was another bright morning and the bloods from the *Constitution* were coming ashore to buy up the rest of Palma. At four the ship was due to leave for Cannes, with at least two extra on board. Once we got on board we had decided to split up. I was going to find a bucket and brush and start scrubbing a few alleyways, the theory being that a man who is busy is almost invisible. If need be, I would keep scrubbing till we got to Cannes. Lawson had other ideas. He felt he could merge better as a blood and would saunter about looking the part. Looking the part wasn't going to be easy for either of us, as by this time we both looked very shabby. My sandals were held together by bits of string. Phillipe's shirt was almost threadbare. Lawson was wearing Andre's shirt and his shoes were passable, so he would stand a better chance than me in passenger accommodation. At about eleven thirty we made our way to the passenger point and waited for the next launch. We had been watching and no-one had been showing tickets or passes. We hung about, waiting our chance and trying to keep a low profile.

Christ! It felt good to be on the water again; so far so good. We had got into the launch separately and hadn't been challenged and now were skimming over the water, the dock receding. Within moments we were beneath the bows of the American liner. It was working! The wake of the launch began to describe a gentle curve until we were pointed back toward the distant dock. The coxswain throttled back and with a gentle bump we pulled alongside the platform. A rope was thrown.

'There you are, ma'am! Okay, sir.' The soft American and uniformed voices, so polite, murmured the passengers by the elbow out of the launch and up the enclosed companionway.

On entering the launch Lawson had immediately fallen into conversation with a group of people and was now ahead of me, halfway up the companionway, helping them carry bags of souvenirs. Once we arrived at the top of the companionway I stepped forward under the canopy and into a foyer that was cool and smelt faintly of cigar smoke. Two uniformed and smiling officers were talking to several passengers just ahead of Lawson, and the line we were in slowed to a halt. What now? I was trying to absorb all the information about me and yet still appear calm. I glanced about; was there a door that I could slip through, perhaps a toilet? Nothing! We were moving forward again and now I was totally focussed on Lawson. How was he going to play this, because play it he had to. One of the officers was questioning him. I strained to hear what was being said. Damn! We were moving forward again, Lawson had been asked to step to one side and the officer was listening to what he had to say but shaking his head from side to side.

'No sir, not at all. I'm sorry you were misinformed, it's not allowed.' Both officers were now giving all their attention to Lawson and hadn't noticed me. Holding my breath and expecting any moment to be challenged I sidled by within a group and there up ahead saw a sign: 'Men's Room'. The cubicle was empty, my luck was holding. I went in and, locking the door, sat down on the toilet. I sat staring at the white tile work, my pulse racing. How long I sat there I don't know. Men came and went, someone tried the door. If only I could stay hidden until we were well clear of Palma.

So Lawson wouldn't be coming to Cannes. Tough! The way things had turned out, though, I couldn't have done it without him. He'd been a pretty good decoy, but I didn't owe him anything. Someone tried the door again. I couldn't sit there forever and would have to make a move soon. The plan was to find the main dining saloon, and then the galley. From there a series of companionways would take me down into the crew accommodation. I would look to find a bucket on the way, there might even be one in a locker outside the cubicle. I'd resolved that as soon as the men's room was empty again I would move.

'Will you be much longer, sir?' It was an American voice and there was a knocking on the door and then unbelievably Lawson's voice.

'Come on, Joe! It's Dave. We have to be off the ship before they ring the police.'

'Come along, sir, let's have you!'

They were polite but firm, even wished us good luck as they put us back in the 'liberty' boat. Having lost his cool, climbed down from his elevated attitude and become more human, Lawson must have known I was planning to murder him. The bastard had squealed on me, he could have stayed shtum and just got off quietly and I would have been on my way. On the dock I went for him and got a good one in but then the gangly bastard managed to hold me off. I'd shaken him though and he even tried to explain but I shouted at him to fuck-off, which he did.

The strange thing about all of this (and I remember it clearly) is that once my anger had subsided and I'd stopped shaking I felt ten feet tall. My plan had been a failure, we still had a trial ahead of us and probably more porridge, but I felt as if I had gained a freedom, freedom from what I'm not sure. Maybe it was because I had tried to do something, I had asserted myself and had stopped feeling a victim.

There were to be many postponements of our trial and we had no option but to cool our heels and be patient. Both Lawson and I spent time separately, even arranging our meals at separate times. He was probably as pissed off at me as I was of him.

The submarine *Cutlass* was part of the US sixth fleet and arrived to moor up in Palma about mid November. The crew, many of whom were about my age, were friendly and interested to hear about my predicament as we met up from time to time in bars and pavement cafes. My smattering of Spanish impressed them and within a short time I had become, if not their pimp, then a go-between between the Mallorcan women on whom they might want to spend their dollars, in return for favours granted. US Ordinary Seaman Frankie Diamond from Minnesota, noticing that I had no warm clothing, very decently loaned me a spare pea jacket as the weather turned chill. He and I became buddies and I was his guest aboard the *Cutlass* for Thanksgiving dinner towards the end of November. The sub was an amazing vessel and despite the crew having to bunk above the torpedo tubes because of the limited space, they had still somehow managed to find room for a coke machine and a jukebox. I was to receive a greater degree of sympathy and hand-outs from the Yanks than I ever got from the Consul's office. The *Cutlass* went back to sea on patrol, and Frankie apologized asking for his pea jacket back. I never saw any of them again. Thanks a lot you guys, whether you ever read this or not. As your playwright Tennessee Williams was to observe, 'The kindness of strangers!'

After a series of delays Lawson and I were finally brought to trial in late November and found not guilty. Anxious to be rid of us and before the court changed its mind, the Consul's office fixed us up with tickets and temporary identity cards and within two days we were boarding the ferry to Barcelona. By this time I had somehow managed to acquire a warmer shirt and a pair of rope and canvas shoes, and Lawson had got hold of a sweater. Our relationship had improved since our argument and I had eventually listened to what he had to say. In a nutshell it was this. We had never admitted our guilt and that was our ace. They never had any evidence on us and that was another ace. If one of us had escaped bail then the court would have taken that as an indication of guilt and would have thrown the book at the one who remained. If I had sailed away on the *Constitution*, Lawson might well still be there. Seeing it from that point of view, wouldn't I have done the same had our positions been reversed?

From Barcelona we took the train travelling north and up through the Pyrenees, then across the border into France. We had a few pesetas, which we changed for francs and with which we bought snacks at various stations when we could. For most of the time we dozed in the warmth of the compartment and for a period I slept in the luggage rack which I found similar to a hammock and very comfortable.

Paris came and went in a rush to change trains and somehow keep warm. Without proper clothing we were more than aware that winter was closing in. Calais, the ferry, and then Dover, England! We didn't get down on our knees and kiss the ground as we thought we would, but in a sort of sleepy daze hurried to get into the warmth of the train taking us to Charing Cross.

Lawson came back with me to Beaufoy Road. Having only experienced each other in alien surroundings, he looked out of place in Aunt Lil's small parlour; perhaps I looked strange to him too. She did us a fry-up and we ate a whole loaf and couldn't stop drinking pot after pot of tea. Time was getting on, the day was beginning to darken and Lawson had to get going. I loaned him an old overcoat that had been my father's which, although much too small for him, would get him to his home somewhere on the south coast. Aunt Lil loaned him his fare and we awkwardly shook hands, arranging to meet in a week's time at Charing Cross station. He didn't turn up and I never saw him again.

Did our experience change us in anyway? I believe it did but it might be difficult to say just how. The world had changed too, particularly Britain's status, which was no longer thought of as 'Great'. The balance of power had altered radically as international condemnation fell upon Eden over his action regarding Suez and Britain was no longer a world power.

On the Beach

1956 was on the wane and I had, with great difficulty, collected my kit-bag with all my belongings from the Company Property office in Southampton, which is worth relating to show the way a Distressed British Seaman (DBS) was treated by the Department of Employment at that time. No seaman liked the term DBS as it conjured up an image of a poor wretch in tears, which was quite the opposite of the image a sea-going man usually held of himself.

Had I explained my problem of getting down to Southampton to collect my gear to the Shipping Federation, then I might have been eligible for a railway warrant. But just how many interviews, subsequent forms to fill in and time would that have taken? Money was my immediate problem, and although Uncle Dick had offered me a loan, I was reluctant to take it because as a family they were only just about getting by and Christmas was almost on us. I accepted a small amount from him for bus fares, but I knew I had savings in the Post Office. The problem was my savings book was with my gear in Southampton. How to retrieve it? Bright Idea! I caught the bus to Waterloo, went to the station master and explained my predicament. He was a decent bloke and having taken down my name and address, he gave me a one-way travel voucher. Presenting myself to the property master at his counter in Southampton, I attempted to claim my kit-bag.

'That white canvas one, pal, there's no lock on it and my Post Office book should be in there. There's about £12 in it and the number is...'

'You got any I.D.?'

'No but...'

'No I.D., no bag!'

'But, but...'

I appealed to him and explained I'd come all the way from London. Could he please phone the Catering Personnel Department and they would have my seamen's registration book, the number of which was R62404? Nope! Would not do. I understood why he was protected behind a wire barrier; otherwise I would have jumped across, throttled him and grabbed my bag. I hadn't eaten since Aunt Lil's breakfast, it was now getting on for three and hunger was gnawing away at me. He went off, made a phone call and came back with the advice that I should present myself at the local dole office to explain my predicament – they didn't close until five o'clock and were only a bus ride away.

At the dole office I waited to see a man, who listened to my story, went away for a long time and came back with forms to fill in. They would find me overnight accommodation and I could present myself tomorrow and they would find me work. Was there any way they could sub me as I was hungry and needed to eat; fish and chips would do? He went off for another long time and returned smiling: Nope! The result was that I was ejected for bad language. What to do? It was getting dark and colder.

Britain is a nation that has been traditionally proud of its Navy, and that pride has been extended to its officers as well, but not to its seaman, even in times of war. Tim Madge in his excellent book *Long Voyage Home* tells of John Cooper, a seaman aboard the first merchant vessel to be sunk by the *Graf Spee* during World War II. He was then subsequently torpedoed three times, a record matched by other seamen. Yet, as had been the case during World War I, their pay was stopped the moment their ship was sunk. Once after being torpedoed close to his home port of Liverpool John was landed back at the pier head and made his way to the shipping office. When he asked the clerk for money to get to his home, the man looked at his records and declared that because of allotments and stoppages he actually owed the company money. John hit him and was arrested.

When his wife found him at the police station she berated him for lying. 'You said you'd been torpedoed, but all the time you've been under arrest.'

You really couldn't make it up, could you? The situation hadn't changed if my experience at Southampton was anything to go by.

At about six-ish I was walking along the main road out of Southampton for London. It was drizzling and with my thumb out, cold, hungry and feeling sorry for myself, I was hoping for a lift. Swish, swish, swish, just keep legging it, but then! A van slowed with the name 'Morley Stockings' on the side and I ran toward it. A window was wound down and the driver leaned across and said, 'Where you going, mate?' 'Anywhere,' I replied. Then the magic words: 'Jump in then.' He was a cheerful bloke, a Londoner and at a guess in his mid thirties. 'I'm going to London, any good to you?' My luck had changed; he was going through Clapham and would drop me off by the Common. We chatted for a bit about this and that before he drew into a transport café. I had pennies in my pocket, enough for a cup of tea, so I went in with him. Maybe he sensed my hunger, I didn't deny it and he ordered us both a massive fry-up and cups of hot sweet tea. It was not the first real act of benevolence shown toward me, as mentioned in the previous chapter, but it was most appreciated and I had to excuse myself to go to the bog so he would not see my tears.

Strange, isn't it? You keep it all together during hard times but then when it's followed by pure human compassion and kindness, it wrings the tears out of you. Well it did me, although I would not have admitted it to a soul then. If I ever knew his name I can't remember it and perhaps that very anonymity allows us to recognize others who are in dire straits and we pass on the benevolence when we can.

He dropped me off at Clapham Common, but before he did he pressed a half crown into my palm and wished me good luck. I walked down Cedars Road in floods of tears. I hadn't been in tears since I was a kid, but after that incident I noticed I was often moved by the movies (such an apt label) and strangely also by the sight of a pregnant woman. Something had gone soft inside me; perhaps I'd discovered my feminine side.

I did eventually get my seaman's book back and that was the key to what funds I had, but I have slim memories of how that transpired. So the P&O had returned my seamen's book, but stamped across my discharge certificate in ink were the words 'Deserted-Palma' which would cause a problem when I tried to find another ship. The Shipping Federation and the Seamen's Union were looking into my case, but taking their time about it. Christmas came and went, Uncle Dick and Aunt Lil were as warm and welcoming over the season as they could be but I felt claustrophobic and restless watching Bruce Forsyth on their telly, and wanted to be away again. My old mate Kenny Daniels had been called up and was now in Malaya with the Seventh Hussars. If I didn't get a result soon and get away to sea once more then I might be joining him; not that I had anything against the Army. I just didn't want to join it.

The New Year, 1957, was almost on us and the big stores were looking for temporary staff to help out with the January sales. It offered an immediate solution to my problem, so for about eight pounds a week I was employed by Barker's of Kensington to stand behind the remnant counter in Basement Fabrics and shout out 'Half the marked price.'

'What are you reading?' an Arts student enquired between shouts. She was at the Guildhall School of Music and, like me, employed by Barker's for the first two weeks of January.

'*The Saint and Mr Teal*,' I replied.

'No, no, I meant what is it you are studying?' she probed.

'Moorish culture,' I said, thinking on my feet and wondering if that would do.

'Oh how wonderful,' she breathed.

'In fact,' I added, 'I've just returned from research on Moorish architecture in Spain.' Her eyes lit up and... well that's another story.

Physical Labour

'You got yourself a bird then?' shouts Len, swinging the van wide. He double-de-clutches then slams her into third and aims for a gap between a stationary bus and a car whose driver is hoping to turn left into Swaffield Road. 'Well ave ya?' His eyes are full on me and he's grinning.

I can't answer. I'm braced, waiting for the crunch of splintered metal, glass and bone. It doesn't happen – not then anyway – and we're through. I let go my fierce grip on the door handle and breathe out. With his foot hard down Len accelerates south along Garrat Lane. I clock the speedo, he's doing nearly fifty. Still, it is the rush hour and we're running late.

'You aving some then?' With his big face grinning he will keep on. It's not so much the questions I mind, I just wish he'd keep his eyes on the bloody road and not on me. I shake my head, willing him to pay attention; we'll be at the lights in Earlsfield soon. Setting him an example, I peer ahead into the early morning fog.

The two weeks work at Barker's just about got me on my feet and after I'd returned Uncle Dick's loan there wasn't a lot left. Looking in the South London press, I'd spotted an opening for a yard labourer, just down the road in Wandsworth. It was the sort of job whereby they might be a bit casual about references and it also had the possibility of an immediate start. A bloke called Nobby took me on, to start the following day. He wanted me there at seven and by getting an early morning workman's bus ticket I was there on time. I'd resolved not to mention anything about Spain or the Merchant Navy, and I lied about my age, saying I was only just 17 and had a year at least to go before call-up, which seemed to fit.

It had taken me a week to tidy the yard up and it was now shipshape and Bristol fashion but had just about knackered me in the process. Nobby, now satisfied that I could graft, started sending me out on site with Tricky and Len. 'On site', according to Len, meant anywhere that wasn't in the yard, but more 'pacifically' as he put it, wherever the job was. First it had been in Croydon but for the past week we'd been in one of those big expensive semis in Burntwood Lane. Tricky was gaffering the job and although time-served as a plumber what he didn't know about sparking and house-bashing wasn't worth knowing. Apart from a complete rewire and redecoration the owners, who were away thank Christ, wanted to add two more rooms in the roof and run a dormer the length of it. 'It's gonna be a piece of piss,' said Len.

***

'If you can keep your head when all about you are losing theirs, then you're a better man than me, Gunga Din,' goes Len. 'That's

Rudyard Kipling,' he adds as I look at him over the rim of my mug. He sips his tea and lets his gaze rest on the steamy window of Fred's Cafe, a greasy spoon in Tooting Bec. He's referring to what happened at the lights in Earlsfield nearly an hour ago. We shouldn't be here in Fred's as we're into customer's time, but because Len forgot two bags of plaster we hadn't got back to the yard till after eight, and as questions were always asked if you were seen there any later than that we'd just nipped in, picked up the plaster and had it away smart-like. Then because of the crash, and all the nonsense with the driver of the Volkswagen, we're not going to get back to the site until gone nine.

'According to this,' says Tricky, tapping the drawing with a brown-nicotined finger, 'they want the dormer at the back, south facing.' There's still an edge to his voice but he has calmed down. He and the driver had just finished unloading a lorry-load of roofing tiles and timber when we'd got back, and he'd really gone into one. Where in the fuck had we been, he wanted to know. Len came clean and put his hands up to forgetting the bags of plaster and our return to the yard. He said nothing, however, about the crash at Earlsfield, or about the police or the ambulance.

'Trouble is,' Tricky says rolling up the drawing, 'the main water tank'll have to come out and it's one of those bleedin' galvanized jobs that takes about eight undred gallons. To move it ain't gonna be easy, right?' His little moustache bristles with the remnants of left-over fury. When we climb up into the loft to have a dekko we can see he is right. By the light of a torch we can see the tank is sat on two wooden beams that disappear through the party wall into next door.

'They'll have to come out as well,' says Tricky. 'Otherwise we can't lay a level floor. Just get stuck in and you'll have it out by teatime. Joe, rig a light up here then start draining the tank off.' I like him saying it like that, it reminds me that I'm part of the team, I nearly salute.

When I first started going out on site with them they had me humping supplies about and mixing sand and cement, that sort of thing. Then once when I was holding a torch for Tricky while he'd connected up a consumer unit, I started asking questions, and he started telling me things. Soon I began to get a sort of map in my head of how things worked. Then within a week or two I was fixing electrical sockets to walls and strangling tube. Mind you, I was still the donkey when it came to the heavy work, but I really didn't mind.

At one o'clock Tricky clears off for lunch and won't be back as he's got to quote on a job over in Kew. The tank's half empty and, by the time Len and I get back from lunch at The Sailor Prince all that's left is a rusty brown sludge in the bottom. Len thwacks it on the side with a meaty fist and the tank hollers back with a galvanized hollow boom.

'Piece a piss,' says Len. 'We'll have it out in no time and it'll be job 'n knock.' It's my job to remove the inlet and ball-cock arrangement but they're rusted on solid. Len squeezes me aside and goes at it with a hacksaw and it all comes away dead easy. Then we both get behind the empty tank and, bracing ourselves against the wall... 'One, two, whe-heh,' shouts Len, as we shove it right off the supporting beams and rush it along the joists to the other side of the roof space. That's the easy bit.

Now Len, particularly after a pint or three, does love a challenge. I'd found that much out on the previous job, over in Croydon. The challenge here is how to get rid of the two supporting beams that stand proud of the joists and disappear into next door. They have to go cos, like Tricky said, they'll be in the way. I'm all for just sawing 'em off shear at the wall, but no, Len says that any job worth doing is worth doing well. He gets like that sometimes. His idea is to loosen them, then drag 'em through to our side. 'Nip down and hand me up the sledgehammer,' says Len, taking his sweater off. 'Then put the kettle on. Thirsty work this.'

From the kitchen I can hear Len hammering away at the beams. He's not tall but chunky built, like the proverbial brick ah... convenience, so it won't take long. The kettle is boiling merrily and I'm just washing out the mugs when the phone rings. It's Tricky. The first thing he tells me is not to touch the beams.

'They might be holding next door's tank,' he shouts, his voice all panicky down the wires. I drop the phone and take the stairs three at a time to meet Len climbing down from the loft.

'That's that job jobbed,' he says, his big face grinning.

'Tricky reckons...' I begin, and then we hear it – and I suppose so does Tricky way over in Kew: a sort of tearing, splitting sound coming from next door. I'd seen a volcano in action but never experienced an earthquake, but it may be similar to what happened: juddering walls, floorboards trembling, showers of dust and bits of ceiling coming down, great chunks of plaster breaking from off the walls and for some reason the landing window shattering. Then into the silence that follows, broken only by the sound of roaring water, Len asks if the tea is ready.

Peering through the ground floor windows into next door we can see the corner of a large galvanized water tank. Identical to the one we have been working on, it's come down all right – not only through their upstairs bedroom but the force has driven it through their lounge ceiling as well. Before our eyes water is cascading in and a footstool is bobbing about. Their settee, however, is not yet totally submerged. We ring the doorbell several times just in case anyone's in and are not fully aware of their problem, but no, they're still at work. After a bit Len looks at his watch, gives it a tap and puts it to his ear.

'S'gone five, better ave it away,' he says. Okay, yeah, it has gone five and the firm won't pay overtime, but it doesn't seem right. Should we leave a note, but then how do you begin? I look at Len and he looks back and shrugs. Strangely silent, we both get into the van and head back to the yard and not once does he go on about whether I'm 'aving some' or not, nor does he even exceed the speed limit.

Len never asked me to keep quiet about the crash at Earlsfield, but it was obvious that if I said anything to Nobby or Tricky then Len would have some quick thinking to do. But then if I said nothing wouldn't I be culpable also? I decided to say nothing unless asked by anyone. There was no explaining to do when we got back to the yard as everyone had left. Len parked the van and locked up but both of us expected some feedback the following morning over the business with the water tank. It seemed too much to hope for that the neighbours would not have noticed anything on their return. If anything we were surprised that Tricky wasn't waiting for us already.

The result of all of this was that when I arrived the following morning Len was already with Nobby and Tricky and I was called in as well. Despite Len's readiness to take the blame for everything we were both immediately sacked on the spot.

Peter Joseph Troy

Another Chance

On a gloomy afternoon in late February I got off the train at Greenhithe in Kent and found my way down to the wharf. The place seemed deserted and apart from a few barges and lighters there were no other vessels in sight. I was supposed to be joining a coal collier called the *Kinnaird Head*, but she'd either sailed or wasn't in yet. Another hour or two it would be dark, but then a voice hailed me. 'You lost, mate?' It came from a stout bloke in a scruffy duffel coat and a balaclava, and he was coiling what looked like a cable.

'Yeah, I'm s'posed to join a collier but...'

'Down the end,' he shouted, pointing toward a jetty, 'right at the end.' I gave him a thank-you wave and wandered off in that direction. Strange, no funnel, no masts, nothing, but he was right. Athwart the jetty end the top rung or two of a ladder projected a foot or so above the decking. I peered down and there it was on a low tide: my future, weighing in at about 2,000 tons. My last ship, the *Iberia*, had been all of 30,000. How the mighty had fallen! I'd walked up gangways, even climbed up ladders, but never had I gone downwards to join a vessel. With rueful thoughts of starting at the bottom again, I swung myself over and down with my bag over my shoulder.

About an hour later, after I'd reported to a bloke called Cliff, who was clad in a boiler suit and beret and who turned out to be the mate, I stood on the shuddering stern-deck as the collier nosed her way past Gravesend and into the Thames estuary. Looking aft and to port, the lights of Tilbury were beginning to twinkle in the dusk of the late afternoon river mist. Ahead of us and to starboard, according to the chart, lay an area marked danger and beyond that lay St Mary's marshes.

The Seamen's Union had come up trumps for me and gained me a chance to redeem myself for past misdemeanours. I was away again but on Home Trade articles this time, and busted back to being a boy rating again: a galley boy, and the only boy on board. But if I proved myself reliable for a time I could get my adult rating back and go Deep Sea again.

The *Kinnaird Head* belonged to a Henry McGregor and was registered in Leith. We were on our way to Sunderland and already there was coal dust beneath my feet and in my hair. I could even taste it. The light was fading and soon I'd have to go below as there were spuds to peel for the crew's supper. The vessel, like many other coastal bulk carriers, was not flat-bottomed as rumoured on account of her tendency to kick up her heels and be lively in relatively calm waters, but she certainly did not seem to like the North Sea as we started northwards up the coast. We didn't steam too far offshore but despite this — and as a result — all crew took great precautions to stay either vertical or horizontal as required. I acquired a long leather strap which it was prudent to use if I didn't want to be hurled from my bunk when attempting to sleep. The mattress beneath me seemed to be alive and breathing as our centre of gravity was constantly and rapidly changing, with the result that I'd never been so active whilst sleeping on my own.

There certainly wasn't any sort of gulf between officers and men, and the departments of Deck, Engine and Catering seemed to be all of a one. I just hoped they didn't expect me to know anything about diesel engines. The rig of the day — every day — for all aboard tended to be black boiler suits and caps or berets. Everyone was on first name terms and cabin inspections seemed to be unheard of. Despite the discomfort I was to enjoy the camaraderie, for almost all of the crew were Geordies and were an easy-going bunch of blokes.

The only indication of whether you were homeward bound or not, home being Tyneside, was whether the coast was to port or starboard. As a galley boy I was to learn a lot about cooking, for the cook, a fat and jolly older man, had spent most of his life working the colliers and had been a galley boy himself. Following his example I first learnt to crack two eggs at a time, sizzle bacon, grill a sausage evenly, boil potatoes and make chip butties. Cookie was always ready with advice and his jollity came with fumes of rum upon his breath. Occasionally there'd be a roast but I never got the hang of making Yorkshire pud. You had to be from the North to do that and if there was a secret to it Cookie wasn't going to tell a Londoner. Of course his readiness to educate me in the world of cuisine had an ulterior motive, as I shall later relate.

Transport of coal from the Tyne to London had been going on since the 12th century, the product was known as 'sea coal' because it arrived by sea. The exposed coal outcrops along the banks of the Tyne at that time were relatively easy to mine, and because the river provided transport of the coal by keelers (flat-bottomed barges) to the coastal colliers waiting offshore, the trade flourished. 'Coals to Newcastle', which I'd sometimes heard referred to now had some significance for me and I was to make many trips up and down England's eastern coast back and forth between the Thames estuary and Tyneside.

Our destinations on the southbound trip were many of the smaller power stations located on coast or river. I remember Little-brook A, B and C, three smaller power stations near Dartford and although I can't be sure now, we may have called at Tate & Lyle's as well. I got to know some of the smaller ports like Swanscombe and Northfleet on the Kent side, where I was sometimes sent ashore to shop for vittles by Cookie.

'Here's a fiver and a shopping list, *hic*. Take this empty onion sack and get a receipt.'

'But, but, hang about, Cookie, we're anchored out, we're not alongside. How am I...'

'Down the rope ladder aft, take the dinghy and I'll tell the mate.'

'But, but...'

'Be back before midday,' Cookie chuckled. 'No later mind, as we'll be underway.' And that was it. He might want stewing steak or more carrots, milk powder or cooking sherry or whatever else he'd suddenly realized we needed for supper that night, by which time we might be off Foulness on a northerly bearing.

Many a seaman has a yarn to tell – it comes with the job – but what if the *Kinnaird Head* could do the same? She might just suffer an identity problem and have as dysfunctional a life as many of the men who were to crew her. Research reveals that her name was only one of many from the time she'd been built in 1944. Launched as the *Empire Peggoty*, she was one of many Empire boats built by the government during the war as Ministry of War Transport (MOWT) vessels, but then contracted out to various shipping lines. Sold to the Harries Bros & Co Ltd of Swansea in 1946, she then became the *Glanrhyd*, but not for long. Sold to the Tavistock Shipping Co of London in 1948 she was then renamed the *Noeldale* but again not for long because in 1949 Henry McGregor of Leith bought her and, with the romantic flair that only the Scots possess, she was renamed *Kinnaird Head* after a north-eastern coastal headland off Fraserburgh.

From 1949 she and her owner remained an item, but then twelve years later, in 1961 and after another divorce, she would be sold on to an Italian, one Gino Giardella, who renamed her *Brick Quinto*. For fifteen years they appear to have got along okay, but then in 1976 she was sold on to the knacker's yard in Savona. Is it any wonder that seagoing vessels are always referred to as 'she'?

It might have been my third, or was it the fourth trip, but like the Woolwich ferry, it was all of a one. We were, I remember, 'anchored out' in the Wear estuary. Some of the crew had gone home for the night and wouldn't be back until morning. It was about 1600 hours and I was on my bunk reading *The Count of Monte Cristo* when Cliff tapped on the cabin door before opening it and put his face round it.

'Cookie's fucking legless, man; can't turn to 'n there'll be four of us wanting our supper. Can you do anything for us, Joe?'

Cookie did like a tot or six, but he could usually do what was required of him and the lads never went hungry. This time though he'd really gone on a bender and was completely rat-arsed. No wonder that he'd been training me up. He'd done it before but everyone had covered for him cos he was a mate, and when he was sober he was a bloody good cook.

'Yeah sure, Cliff, I'll have a go, a fry-up okay?' I said, swinging myself off my bunk.

'Anything man, anything,' replied Cliff.

There was a problem, however, because Cookie had the key to the pantry locker, had barricaded himself in his cabin and was telling anyone who tried to reason with him to piss off. I didn't know where he kept the key so a fry-up was out of the question. Still I had an idea and went and saw Cliff who agreed. Twenty minutes later found me rowing the dinghy ashore with an empty onion sack and a whip-round of cash. It was dark when I got back with five portions of cod and chips, a jar of pickled onions and twelve large bottles of Guinness. We all sat in the mess by lamplight and it had to be one of the best nights I can remember, the stories and jokes going around. Light from oil lamps gimballed to the bulkheads have their own mysterious quality and seemed to add flavour to old seagoing yarns. Anchored out with all engines stopped and our navigational and working lights fuelled by oil, it was easy to imagine ourselves back in time.

Back in the cabin later, in my bunk and the time gone midnight, I was deep into Dumas's novel, reading by oil-lamp. My surroundings and the tale had me really transported when something strange happened. It was the only supernatural experience that I ever encountered and for some reason I did not at first feel any fear.

The lamp began to dim and then went out, which was surprising because I had earlier trimmed the wick and topped up the oil. Apart from only a dull gleam coming through the porthole and no other sounds, there then began a rattling of the matches in their box upon the ledge. It was not continuous but would stop and start, sometimes louder, sometimes quieter. Deciding not to investigate, I slipped down beneath the covers. But then I began to be fearful that something might physically touch my face so I got deeper and deeper underneath and lay listening to the intermittent shaking of the matches. They did eventually stop and I fell asleep.

Not wanting to sound stupid, I said nothing about my experience but over the next few days I began to refer to haunting generally, thus giving anyone the chance to mention if anything had ever bothered them. But I drew a blank. Was it the Guinness? I don't think so, but who can say?

After about two months on the collier I was eager to get back Deep Sea and to recover my adult rating. I had every reason to think that my discharge would be a V.G. (very good), and that would cover over my earlier V.N.C. (voyage not completed). Hopeful that my probation could be ended, I arranged to be paid off when next we arrived back at Swanscombe.

To Africa!

The Union Castle Shipping Company owned many cargo-passenger vessels and sailed regularly to Cape Town. The return trip took approximately ten weeks and was popular with seamen for many reasons: regular overtime, those who were married and did not want to be away for longer, the many exotic ports the ship called at and the fact that once you were through the Suez Canal, you were only at sea for a few days at a time. It was also a clockwork service sailing every Thursday afternoon at 4.00 pm from Southampton or London. 'Follow the Swallows,' proclaimed the Company's publicity.

Once it had cleared the Thames and the English Channel, giving Biscay as wide a berth as possible and with the Iberian Peninsula to port, the vessel steered a course for the straits of Gibraltar, then through the Pillars of Hercules and into the calmer waters of the Mediterranean. With North Africa to starboard and on an easterly bearing past Benghazi it would only take a day or two until the skipper hung a right and made for Suez.

Through the Red Sea, between Africa and Asia, around the Horn of Africa and down the African Coast was a pleasant enough journey and also gave all those making the trip a chance to escape the British winter. No wonder it was popular. Ten weeks was also a fair spell away for those who perhaps had generated an interest by Scotland Yard into their recent activity. By sailing as crew their names would not be on any passenger list and they wouldn't need a passport if they had a seaman's book.

The first ports to be called at were those of what then was British East Africa: Mombasa, the island of Zanzibar and then returning to Dar-es-Salaam on the coast. From there the vessel continued south to call first at Beira, then Lourenco Marques, which were ports located in Portuguese East Africa. We'd then hug the coast down to South Africa, calling in at Durban, East London, Port Elizabeth and eventually Cape Town. Plenty of bronzy, plenty of overtime and what wasn't there to like?

During the fifties it wasn't unusual to see an ad in the London papers offering those who were inclined to apply the opportunity to sign on as a steward or waiter, preferably on the basis of having relevant experience. Many professional waiters from the big London hotels and restaurants did sign on as the Union Castle Shipping Company seemed always desperate for catering crew, although personal appearance and intelligence would not be compromised. Depending on the desperation of the company's catering department, if a man didn't have experience but could pass for being a Homo Sapiens, and could count to ten, well the company would train him up for an hour or so. Standards had to be maintained! As a result you might find yourself working with what transpired to be a motley crew.

There was 'Little Jim' I well remember; he was a short-arse but had a deep voice and drew attention to himself by addressing a passenger at his table thus: 'Marrer, mate. You want marrer?'

We found out later that before being accepted he'd driven a coal lorry and had only seen the Company's ad in the *Evening Standard* on the previous Friday. We wingers took him on and put him right, teaching him spoon, fork and silver service in the stewards' mess. Quite what the Seamen's Union thought about such hirings is anyone's guess; perhaps they weren't aware. I don't ever remember anyone asking me for my Union Card: 'Closed Shop? What you on about?'

On the 17th April 1957 I boarded the *Dunnotar Castle* in the Victoria Docks and signed ship's articles for a ten-week run to the Cape. British and French troops had been evacuated in December of the previous year from Suez after a massive cock-up, and Israeli troops had left just a month before, during March: the Canal was open for business as usual. My job as a waiter, or winger, in tourist class found me attempting to serve two sittings of fourteen bloods for each meal. Two tables of seven had to be laid and re-laid for at least three courses. It was my first trip as a fully fledged winger.

All waiters, whether in first class or tourist, were expected to know the basics of waiting at table. How to lay a table with whatever cutlery is required in the right order from the outside of the cover: soup spoon, fish, main, dessert and steady as you go. The ability to offer silver service with spoon and fork was a requirement. Serve food to the left and wine or water to the right of the blood. Then there's the etiquette of giving a 'Sir' or 'Madam' where required in a soft voice and, if you can manage it, with a smile. It wasn't difficult, but I had braced myself for this first meal. If all fourteen came in together would I be able to keep their orders in my head? Some were going to want the potage, others the consommé. There were a variety of courses and they had a choice. How do you carry fourteen plates? What if they were late? I had an hour to get them in and out and lay up for the next sitting. Bloody hell, could I cope?

The Ginger bloke serving on the next station to mine during that first meal gave me a hint: do one table at a time, he'd said. He seemed relaxed enough and had the right attitude. If I watched him I'd soon get the hang of things.

I was lucky that first lunchtime. Passengers appeared in twos and threes. Two men sat at one of my tables and a woman went to the other so I sat her first, pulling out her chair and filling her glass with iced water. I zipped out with their orders and had the three of them started before three others came in. Maybe things weren't so bad. The meal began to progress but Ginger's lot hadn't appeared. When they did, five minutes later, all fourteen came in together. Led by a fat bloke, they sat themselves at his tables. Although I was busy I made myself observe how Ginger would handle things, rather him than me. He didn't attempt to seat any of them, not even the women, but just stood there leaning up against his dummy, his legs crossed and with a matchstick between his teeth. He waited until they'd got themselves sorted and they'd looked at the menu. When they looked up expectantly toward him, Ginger had his cue and without moving called out 'Ands up for soup!'

If I was startled I need not have been because his bloods did just that, and he didn't give any of them a choice. They all got potage which he had already brought in: fourteen soup plates sat piled up and sandwiched between dinner plates already on his dummy.

'When all else fails lower your standards,' a wise man once said – it was either Schopenhauer or Max Bygraves. I can't be sure but I was to realize later that it is a truism that applies to many situations in life. If standards in the saloon were not maintained then the Headwaiter and Chief Steward had to be somewhat philosophical about it as we had sailed without a full complement of saloon staff in tourist class. Like the other wingers I had two sittings of fourteen, but had we not been short-handed then it would have been two sittings of ten. So okay let's be flexible here, maybe it is a workup but we were getting two hours overtime daily at time and a half and that could mount up over six weeks. The union had a name for it: The Utilisation of Manpower or in common parlance 'Cut me some slack, and I'll do the same.'

I paid off the *Dunnotar Castle* with a healthy pay packet and having liked the trip decided I'd stay with the Company, if not the ship. I'd apply for a trip on the *Warwick Castle*, sailing some weeks later and give myself a month of summer ashore in London. With a bit of luck and a following breeze I might find a girlfriend. After that first trip I was to make another six trips to the Cape in succession and didn't return to the New Zealand coast until early in 1959. Maybe it was because I was really beginning to enjoy what London had to offer when on leave and I didn't want to be absent for too long.

'Ziss-one-an-earner-then?' The *Warwick Castle* was only a few hours into the channel – about fourteen miles south west off Plymouth and abeam the Eddystone light. It was an Essex voice and freely translated its owner was enquiring if this ship was an earner. Although many seafarers were lacking any entrepreneurial ambitions or skills, there were those who went away to sea not for the lifestyle or the crack of it, but to earn the dosh. If you were going to be away for ten weeks with nothing but an ocean to look at, well you may as well get some in and overtime became important. The Essex voice may have had a large family to keep, or an eye for a nice motor, perhaps a Jag. With such priorities then a conflict with management was in the making.

The Union Castle Shipping Company and its shareholders were also interested in whether the vessel was an earner, but its directors would have articulated the question differently to the Essex voice. Their cost accounting department in Fenchurch Street would have been aware of the catering department's wage bill for every vessel belonging to the company.

So what exactly is the catering bill for the *Warwick Castle* each trip compared with her sister ship, the *Durban Castle*? The question would have the potential for an illuminating answer as both vessels were of similar tonnage, carried the same complement of crew, the same number of passengers and made identical voyages to the Cape.

'Good Lord, old man! That's almost double,' might have spluttered Puffy Jenkins, one of the directors of the company, when given the figures. 'Who's the purser on the *Warwick*? What's the fellow's name? Not old Ridler, is it?' he could ask, accepting a large pink gin in the company bar. Conflict in the making? You'd better believe it, brother!

'Is it then, is it an earner?' Essex was eager for an answer, throwing the question wide to a small group of us on the foc'sle before we went down to lay up tables for dinner.

'Well it was last trip – plenty of bubble,' said Johnny Bull, out of Dagenham. 'But they've got rid of old Ridler and it'll be touch and go with this new geezer off the *Durban*. We'll see'. And we did. A notice in the stewards' mess the following day cleared up any misunderstanding.

'OVERTIME'

**All overtime in future will only be paid
IF sanctioned beforehand by the Second Steward.
Signed. Gordon Brown (Purser)**

Stewards and waiters, if memory serves me right, worked a fifty-six hour week over seven days, which was an eight hour day: time enough to serve two sittings of ten for three meals a day. But when you added in the utility duties to keep the brass polished, the passenger accommodation scrubbed and cleaned and the early morning beer carries to keep the bar stocked, not to mention the mandatory emergency and lifeboat drills, it was more likely to be a ten-hour day, which meant fourteen hours a week at time and a half, thus equal to an extra twenty-one hours per week. Therefore make a ten-week trip to the Cape and back, and your pay-off would include another 210 hours plus Sundays at Sea. Okay, even after deductions it meant a decent leave ashore, also enough to buy the baby a bonnet or stump up a deposit for the E-Type. Without the overtime it was a straight £28 a month plus all found. It sounds paltry now but back in the fifties that was the going rate. Factory work at that time, with overtime, might earn a man £10 weekly to keep a family on.

Even so, if you were going to be away from friends and family – what later would be termed unsocial hours – then the overtime became important if you were to keep the missus happy or eventually keep up the payments on the motor.

You didn't have to be a Marxist or even a sea-lawyer to recognize the age-old potential for conflict. Seamen were of course unionized. The National Union of Seamen did a good job in the UK, but unlike shore-side work who was to represent you whilst you were at sea? I never remember anyone volunteering to be a delegate or shop steward. Besides what action could be taken? Working conditions on board ship were governed by the Board of Trade, and employers had to ensure that such conditions were observed. If a grievance arose then a man could not strike for that would be mutiny: a punishable offence. It didn't mean being strung from the yard-arm but it did mean it wouldn't be sorted until you got back to your home port. In our case that would be ten weeks, but many companies could keep their ships and crew away for up to two years. Time enough for a grievance to fester and chaos to erupt.

The Essex voice, whose owner turned out to be a bloke called Micky Payne, had a florid face that seemed pasted onto a coconut, and he was pissed off. He wasn't the only one. Many had joined or returned for another trip expecting the overtime payment that had been paid on previous trips on the *Warwick* to be honoured. Something had to be done, and it was - more of which later.

***

The Suez Canal did not have the same allure for me as the Panama Canal, with its jungle, wildlife and exciting runs ashore.

Suez was bleak, arid and, despite its bum-boats and gilly-gilly men, had little appeal. Mention Suez and most people immediately think of the crisis that changed Britain's status as a world power and showed up what was referred to as our 'Special Relationship' with Uncle Sam for what it was - a myth.

Built by De Lesseps, a Frenchman, and opened in 1869, the canal was owned by a consortium known as The Suez Canal Company. Its shareholders were France, Egypt and Britain. With France being the major shareholder, it became strategically important immediately as it was the shortest link from Europe to the Indian Ocean. Access to the Persian Gulf, India and the scramble for Africa became easier in terms of distance, time and cost. But then six years later Egypt - as part of the Ottoman Empire - had debts they could not settle and Disraeli's Government agreed to pay four million pounds for Egypt's shares. Britain's shares, although at the time not a controlling interest, were now 45% and that upset the French.

Upsetting the French had become a British habit over the centuries but upsetting the catering crew on the *Warwick Castle* was something else. 'No overtime regardless' seemed to be the Second Steward's last word on the matter but that didn't stop the bollockings that followed when several wingers failed to turn to for the morning beer carry. 'Ok Guv!' was the response. 'We'll turn to for the beer carry but forget the scrub-outs and the brass. If we're maintaining an eight-hour day, you can't have it both ways.'

'So,' said Brown, the new purser in his office, 'they're now refusing orders, are they? Then we'll have them up on the bridge. A few loggings will change their mind.' Given the purser's background in the Royal Navy there were those who thought he might have wished for floggings rather than loggings. Whatever the outcome, the distinction between being a company man or not caused some polarity of feeling. You couldn't blame a man for attempting to maintain his position on a career path set by the company. Without a proper representative to state his case a man could be seen as a trouble-maker and his name could have been underlined in red on a list in the company's offices: zilch goes any idea of promotion.

Before we got to Mombasa several stewards had been before the Old Man, who had listened to their grievances. He hadn't logged anyone but had threatened to if they didn't carry out their duties. His advice was to keep a log of all hours worked, and then take it up with the company and the seamen's union on our return, which seemed sensible, but with no guarantee of being paid for any overtime worked.

Mombasa, in modern day Kenya, is a small island off the East African coast and has had a bloody history. In the 16th century the Portuguese attacked, looted and razed the place to the ground many times before taking control and completing Fort Jesus in 1593. As a fort one wonders if it was fit for purpose for it changed hands about nine times before the British finally took control in 1875 and turned the place into a prison.

Going ashore with the lads on the many times I called there, I wouldn't then have been aware of the foregoing facts as I had different interests: a few hours ashore wouldn't have been time enough to indulge in such historical research anyway, particularly as the heat made us impatient to find the nearest bar and have a look at the natives – preferably the female variety. It certainly didn't have the flavour of Panama City and apart from a few hangovers there were not many problems to take to the doc when the ship left the port.

Making numerous trips to the Cape and back on various of the company's vessels, it's difficult to recall exactly what ship I was on – it could have been the *Dunnotar*, the *Warwick*, or was it the *Durban Castle*? But it was in Mombasa that an incident occurred that leaves me with a pungent memory. It didn't become a matter for record so I can't date it.

I had been making my way back to the ship about midnight and there was no hurry as we weren't due to steam away until about midday. I decided to return before the others in the Star bar, not because I was skint as there was always the 'tarpaulin muster' (we all threw whatever change we had left into a kitty) to rely on, but an early night was always a good idea.

To get back to the ship on the proper and safe path involved walking two sides of a long triangle so it made sense to take the shortcut, the hypotenuse, which happened to be through low bush and scrub adjacent to the jungle. Although it was a well-used track by locals and seamen during the day I wouldn't have chanced it had the moon not been nearly full. Wild animals, it was reputed, were as anxious to avoid us as we were them so the trick was to make a noise if you were making your way across alone, perhaps whistling or even singing, thus giving any snakes or maybe the odd gorilla or large cat a warning that you were approaching so they wouldn't mess with you.

Nothing too dramatic happened but coming toward me was a bedroom steward called Spinney, an Irishman.

'Is it yourself, Joe?' he asked. 'Ah wouldn't you be after knowing it, but I got cot for late duty,' he said, 'and here I promised to see some people.' He tapped the side of his nose and gave me a wink. 'You want to come along? Should be a laugh, c'mon, now.' I began to tell him I was skint but...

'You won't be after needing the shekels where we're going,' he laughed. He was a funny bloke, funny ha-ha I mean and thus good company, so I thought yeah, why not? Spinney had made many trips to this coast and knew his way about so it wasn't long, whilst walking back toward the Star bar, before he took a diversion off the track and into the jungle with me following. Within five minutes I smelt smoke, then spotted lights, a fire and several mud huts within a clearing. Two or three figures emerged from the shadows, which gave me a bit of a turn but didn't bother Spinney. He had packets of something that crackled tucked within his shirt and offered them over. I don't know what they were but it brought forth large white-toothed smiles and a clap on the shoulder for us both. Inside the mud hut, because that was what it was, with a conical roof, a lamp hanging in the centre gave off enough light to see the natives more clearly, all blokes, and we were offered what felt like straw-filled sacks to sit upon.

There wasn't a lot of talk but mimes and gestures had us all drinking sweet and sour hooch that Spinney explained to me was a brew of onion beer. It wasn't long before he got passed a pipe and taking his time over a few puffs and pleasant sighs, he then passed it on to me. I had never been a smoker so took a few cautious drags that rasped the back of my throat and set me off coughing. Amongst the laughs that came forth were a giggle or two, and a slim black arm with bangles around the wrist reached over my shoulder with a gourd and I was bid to drink. The water was surprisingly cold and set me right. I had another drag or three and feeling as if I was somehow a character out of a movie or maybe a book, perhaps *Alan Quartermain,* I entered into the spirit of it all.

Then the singing and gentle drumming began, like nothing that I'd heard of before, a high and low humming and drumming and what I can only describe as throat clicking by the men, and also the women who were clearly present but reclining further back along the walls of the hut. My hair, which was quite thick at the time, seemed to hold some sort of fascination for them and fingers were in it, gently tugging and stroking, which was a pleasant enough sensation. More onion beer was offered and around the pipe came again.

'Are you right, Joe?' said Spinney, before he burst forth with a harmonica into *'I'll take you home again Kathleen'*.

'I'm as right as the mail,' said I recalling my Irish father's phrase from childhood. And I was, too, for Spinney seemed at that moment to be family, he and I might have come from the same Celtic tribe back in history. I was aware of the pipe coming round more often than the onion beer and Spinney accompanying me with his harmonica as I sang *'If you were the only girl in the world'*, before everything went wobbly...

Later I had an impression of soft skin and crinkly hair, the smell of coconut oil, more hair attention and being cuddled and returning the favour before periods of oblivion had me waking from a dream of someone sandpapering my left buttock. It brought me to, with daylight piercing through the opening of the hut and the smell of wood smoke and coffee, and a goat that was licking my arse. Spinney was still at it, I could hear his harmonica and voice outside…

'*Paddy McGinty, an Irishman of note, fell into a fortune and thought he'd buy a goat…*' which seemed to be the right song under the circumstances. A mug of the coffee was brought into me by a young girl who was wearing earrings that appeared to be made out of Liquorice Allsorts. On closer inspection that is exactly what they were. Spinney, it was clear, knew the score. He told me later that he'd bought then from Woolworths in East Ham, and first brought them over two trips ago and not only had the tribe enjoyed the taste, but baking them in the hot sun, they'd made them into brooches, earrings and necklets which were now in demand.

Spinney got us both back before 'turn-to'. No time for a shower before we did the mandatory scrub-outs, but later shampooing my hair I found a souvenir from my hours in the mud hut: minute coloured beads had been woven tightly into the hair above my ears, which I could only remove with scissors before serving breakfast with a weird haircut. Thinking back on that night, I felt somehow bonded with everything: Spinney, the jungle, the sounds, my hosts and even the goat. Whatever it was that I smoked that night began some nurturing of my soul and that is about the only way I can describe it.

The ship left Mombasa at midday as scheduled. A few passengers had disembarked and others had joined.

'Have you seen her – on Johnny Bull's table?'

'Christ give me twenty minutes with her.'

'Twenty minutes! Leave it out, she'll see to you in five.'

'Have I seen her? You'd have to be blind not to.'

'What a darling...the knockers...not many like that to the pound.'

The lads were almost spilling their seed in describing her in the plate-house and Bully was made up. She was a stunning looking blonde who seemed more than happy to display her natural charms: tight white shorts, a sunny disposition and plenty of cleavage which John could take advantage of from his elevated position when serving her. She was travelling alone to Durban and had a double cabin all to herself. We learnt this from Bimbo, her bedroom steward, who lived up to his name as he liked to camp and mince about. Further information revealed the blonde was a Miss Van-der-Broek and up in the bar on B deck she became very popular with those men who were travelling alone and with whom she shared her company.

Within a day or two we tied up in Dar-es-Salaam, which if I recall correctly was like a sort of equatorial Torquay but less dangerous and sold only vanilla ice cream. It was there we took on deck cargo and a few passengers disembarked. Tanzania had not gained its independence then, and didn't until 1963, when Julius Nyerere became Prime Minister, so Dar-es-Salaam may well have changed from my recall of it.

'And get this,' said Micky Payne in the stewards' mess. He'd become really resentful about the withdrawal of overtime and was banging on about it again, reminding us several times to keep a log of our hours and how we all ought to refuse to sign off when back in London until we had met with the union delegate. He was right, of course, but he was also living up to his surname by being a pain in the proverbial.

'And get this,' he announced louder so he had our full attention. 'All second stewards get a bung if they not only keep the bubble down but the ship arrives back in London with minimum loss of crockery, cutlery and silverware. So we know what to do, right?'

As a result the sea bed between the coast and Zanzibar began to resemble the kitchen department of Fortnum and Mason's, and the Second Steward began to look unhappy. If someone in some future millennium ever pulls the plug on the seabed of the Indian Ocean and it all drains away, then marine archaeologists of that time will find soup tureens, ladles, coffee pots, milk jugs and cutlery all with what appear to be hieroglyphics such as *U.C.S.Co* engraved upon them. Will they be able to decipher what it stands for? Or more importantly, how such trove came to be there with no evidence of a 20th-century ship wreck, and why? Well because an official of the shipping company decided to cut the stewards' overtime.

Zanzibar was magical with its Sultan's Palace, which had enormous studded doors to withstand elephant attack and where it was reputed that the Sultan still kept a harem. Before the ship came within sight of the island you could smell the cloves wafting across the sea on a warm breeze. Miss Van-der-Broek had been there several times and she slipped Johnny Bull a fat tip. We learnt later that she never went ashore but seemed to entertain several men, one after the other, in her cabin. It was a practice she continued until she disembarked at Durban to join the *Cape Town Castle*, travelling back up the coast to Mombasa where she repeated the circuit time and again on the company's vessels, thus making a lot of males happy, earning herself a lot of money and having a nice lifestyle.

Johnny Bull was heartbroken when he found out she was on the game. He really thought she had the hots for him, not just because she was so very nice but also because she flirted with him, caressing his thigh beneath the table cloth when he was up close whilst offering silver service with a spoon and a fork. He told me later over a drink that he'd actually mastered the art of serving the peas one at a time.

Because I made many trips to South Africa, which involved calling at all ports of call there and back, it means that I was back and forth ashore to each port for a total of perhaps a dozen times. My recollections of each trip, as mentioned earlier, are confused. There were, for instance, many Miss Van-der-Broeks plying their trade up and down the coast and just as many Johnny Bulls who lost their hearts to them. Likewise there would have been other Mickey Paynes, but not many Irishman like Spinney: he was a one off, but my experiences were not unique.

Beira and Lourenco Marques, further south, were then in Portuguese East Africa. The latter, now renamed Maputo, is the capital of what became today's Mozambique after independence in 1975. During the times that I was there I witnessed what I thought were prisoners working the docks. Harshly treated by gang bosses they were often beaten with a cane, which was enough to upset many seamen and incidents occurred. The workers were not in fact prisoners but forced labourers; a system of conscription was in force whereby young men between certain ages were forced into categories of employment such as the mines, plantations and the docks.

To see one man beating another was too much for Simpson, an engineer's steward. Standing on the well-deck when he observed the abuse, he shot down the gangway in a rage and went for the gang boss wielding the cane; snatching it from the man, he set about thrashing him. There followed an uproar and men in uniform rushed forward. Simpson was restrained but not before he was bloodied himself. The first mate and another two officers went down to sort it out and a long meeting ensued. The Port authorities, we learnt later, were all for taking Simpson away and locking him up, and it was only after money and bribes changed hands that we sailed with Simpson on board. Up until that time he was just one of the guys, mildly spoken and easy to get on with. His cuts healed and he continued in the same way. He became nonetheless one of my heroes for having the balls to do what he did. Somewhere in England he's now probably someone's grand-dad, changing nappies and maybe tending his tomatoes.

At the time it would not have occurred to many of us, but on reflection didn't Simpson's actions typify the discontent or hostility that prevailed between the neighbouring imperial powers; between one European colonial authority and another? The British, Italians, Portuguese and Dutch shared the East African coast, and apart from the early rivalries for trade it was the British who would assume the moral high ground for being the first to condemn and eventually abolish the slave trade. In contrast to the Afrikaans control of South Africa and the Portuguese control further north there existed no apartheid in British controlled East Africa and it was therefore always a relief to be back in Mombasa, Dar-es-Salaam or Zanzibar.

***

'Speaking of fiddles,' said Bottle-brush, an older guy who was the utility and glory-hole steward, 'I know a bloke, name of Wol, out of Limehouse, who had a smooth one running and had been doing it for years. Mind you, he had to return again and again on the same old tub up to Gdansk on the Baltic.' We were jugging back ginger squares in the Playhouse in Durban and the yarns were flowing as much as the liquor. Someone, his name now evades me, had just finished a tale that involved painting sparrows yellow and selling them as canaries. Bottle-brush, or B-B for short, who was in his fifties and had seen service during the war, had our attention as he often had a way of telling a yarn that would in another lifetime have put him on the stage.

'Poland is a strong Catholic country,' he continued, 'and French letters are hard to come by, no pun intended. Well Wol found himself ashore there and looking for a bit of the other, he picked up a whore. Now Wol was cute and never went anywhere without a packet or two of johnnies, for fear of catching the clap as he was married. Having completed the dirty deed the woman then made him an offer he couldn't refuse. For the rest of the packet, she'd give him a free one when he got his breath back.' B-B paused at this point and looked meaningfully at his empty glass, which was hurriedly topped up. We were all ears and gave him a respectful moment whilst he took a long draught.

'So Wol decided on a return trip, which was only about a week's turn around,' he went on. 'During that time he bought as many packets of Durex as his pay-off would allow. Mind you, it caused a few raised eyebrows in his local chemist but that didn't bother Wol. Anyway he made so much profit and had so much sex that when he got back from Gdansk he had to go on a high protein diet with plenty of zinc picolinate. There was a snag, however: the Polish zloty wasn't a currency easy to change into sterling at the time, so to enjoy the proceeds he could only spend it in Poland.' He broke off for a moment and took another swig, wiped his mouth and said, 'Have you seen some of those Polish bints? Fucking gorgeous and stacked. Christ, I wish I were younger.'

With such a story a few minds were made up by those enjoying the yarn: what companies run to the Baltic? How much discount if you could buy Durex by the hundredweight? Not wanting to let the story go but to hear more of Wol, one of us went up to the bar to get another few jugs in. It turned out that over the years Wol became a wealthy man in Gdansk with a big bank account, as many women as he wanted and a smart rented flat. He'd moved on from supplying prophylactics to the Polish population and had discovered a thriving black market for dentist drills.

'So where is he now?' someone asked B-B.

'Well last time I saw him he'd put on a lot of weight and looked like Fatty Arbuckle. Mind you, I did hear he died shortly after that, quite young he was, only forty-six but he probably died on the job, and happy with three women in his bed.' B-B took another long draught and then finished the story with a wink, saying, 'Mind you, it might have been something he ate.'

***

The Playhouse in Durban and the Navigator's Den in Cape Town were the bars to hang out in. They were fairly up market and you were supposed to wear a tie. There were plenty of women but they all seemed to be accompanied by huge blokes with blonde hair and wearing rugby blazers so we didn't really get a look in. We couldn't get involved with the black women of course, because of the apartheid laws and I never enjoyed time ashore in South Africa.

Something of a sad curiosity was a character on the wharf in Cape Town, who had to rely on hand-outs from various crews if he was to continue to exist. We knew him as 'Snowball' and nature had played a nasty trick on the poor bloke for he wasn't black or white but had Negroid features with patches of white and black skin – making him a sort of piebald – and it was reputed that he wasn't accepted by blacks or whites.

If you did go ashore in Cape Town you were warned not to go into an area called 'District Six' as it was quite likely that you may not come out. The warning never stopped Fletcher though. In he went and sure enough he never came out.

Quite a few blokes never made it back home over the years from their time at sea and for numerous reasons. One that comes to mind, although it could have been hearsay, was a jumped-up Kentish man by the name of Pat Coles who was the Second Waiter on one of the company's vessels. He was apparently a bit of a stand-over-man, who would regularly bollock blokes in a loud voice, ordering them to redo their scrub-out or re-polish the brass. He liked to humiliate a man in front of others and would often delay him when off ashore, usually with some petty grievance or other, just to flex his authority. These kind of blokes - and you do meet them everywhere - usually have an idea who they can try it on with, but Colesy seemed to lack the ability to 'read' certain people and clearly picked on the wrong man. As mentioned earlier there were a few moody's keeping a low profile and escaping London for a bit until whatever heat that they had engendered with Scotland Yard had cooled down, and if you had any sense you could pick out those who didn't welcome too many questions, and so you minded your business and kept schtum. Anyway, so the story goes, Colesy threatened to take this particular moody up onto the bridge and in front of the skipper for refusing to do something or other. Moody, not wanting any awkward publicity, caved in and did what Colesy ordered, but it must have rankled. The night before the ship got back to London – Channel Night it was – Colesy goes missing. He never turned to and just as they were off the Lizard the following morning, it was discovered his bunk had not been slept in. He never reappeared and the police became involved, asking questions. Just another mystery that probably remains an open file in some dusty archive.

The *Warwick Castle* had begun her return, north up the coast with fresh bloods and cargo and calling into the same ports. For whatever reason there were fewer passengers and so the catering crew had it easier – only two sittings of eight on my tables and many cabins empty. With more time on our hands we were more relaxed and took time out to play pranks on each other and be flirtatiously dead-pan cheeky to the female bloods, particularly at meal times.

'Would Madam like a leek?' 'Would Madam like stuffing?'

You had to be aware, too, if anyone had been 'at' your table before the meal and during your absence. Had someone loosened the tops to your condiments? Had they replaced salt for sugar? Had someone stitched the prongs of a fork to the tablecloth? Had someone been at the pickled onions in their jar on the main dummy and threaded them like conkers? On occasion a winger might return to find his fully laid up table for two unbolted from its fixings, carried into the lift and sent up to A deck. 'Excuse me, Guv, but someone's nicked my table' would be his lament to the headwaiter.

'Go on, I dare you.'

'Yeah, how much?'

'Half a crown.'

'You're on.'

And we'd all wait for it; mind you he'd make it look good... preferably if the vessel had a nice roll to it. Entering from the galley revolving door, your man would have his tray piled high with two columns of plates and chop covers. Halfway through the saloon he'd hesitate as first one of the columns would begin to lean dangerously to port. To remedy this he'd tilt his tray, thus causing the other column to tilt to starboard. If he was really good his actions would continue cabaret-like with many bloods and wingers in frozen observation until the inevitable happened. When it did, and a loud crash resulted, noisy cheering could be heard from the galley.

With fewer passengers you'd expect it would have been easier to keep abreast of personal chores: you could do your dhobi more often and your shoes could be more highly polished. It didn't seem to work that way. Instead I became less energized. The less I had to do, the less I wanted to do and others seemed to have become the same. We'd suddenly realize it was the Captain's weekly inspection at eleven and the cabin you shared with three others had become a real kharsi– bunks unmade, books and magazines strewn around the place, ashtrays overflowing, apple cores and plum stones that had been used as ammo everywhere, someone's discarded vest and maybe a dirty cup or two, plates, empty lager bottles. A flurry of activity resulted before the Old Man appeared with the Mate and the Doctor. Locker doors and drawers were opened and all of the above flotsam and jetsam stuffed in wherever it could go regardless of whose locker or drawer it belonged to. Bunks were rapidly made, sweeping, scrubbing, dusting, and hiding completed just as the Old Man arrived. We stood breathlessly to attention, praying that he wouldn't open a locker door, because if he did he'd be showered upon with everything wedged and balanced inside.

The trick was to leave something that would draw his attention and cause him to remark upon, and with luck he'd inspect no further.

'That mirror needs a shine – see to it!'

'Yes Sir!' with a click of the heels. Then he and his little team would be gone and we'd make faces behind his back.

'Mr Polythene' would have been horrified to share a cabin with such riff-raff. He'd got his nickname by his habit of setting up his personal ironing board in the mess almost every night after B-B had tidied up after our evening meal. There he'd be in perfectly ironed shorts and whiter than white T-shirt. His thick raven-black hair, which we all secretly envied, had been brushed and coiffed, not a hair out of place – ever. With a flawless olive skin and pearl-like molars he would proceed to iron his socks with great care. The finished articles then would be folded, pressed and slipped into one of a supply of small polythene bags.

No one took the piss because even a mild acknowledgement of his activity would cause an amused rising of his perfectly trimmed left eyebrow, and you would not want to be the subject of the cutting put-down that he had a reputation for.

This legend was a lounge steward. Correction: he was 'The Lounge Steward par excellence' and Liberace, in comparison, looked like Norman Wisdom. There was a rumour that he might be some sort of alien because nobody ever saw him eat or go ashore, although he had been noticed in the stewards' ablutions wearing a shower cap. Had he camped about like Bimbo then he could have been categorized. But no, he was just 'Mr Polythene' and was extremely popular with the blue-rinsed matrons in the Lounge for he knew his Shakespeare and would – if prevailed upon – recite a sonnet or a monologue. Furthermore he'd display his virtuosity on the grand piano which, among other of his other duties, he kept highly polished and tuned.

***

There we were in flip-flops with just a towel in place because of the heat. We'd carried our mattresses out onto the hatch covers where we'd sleep the night under the bowl of bright stars whilst they worked their magic on us, or listen to voices offering their take on current affairs, whilst having a last smoke at the rail.

'Farouk, yeah, that's the geyser, he owned the canal before our lot went in and got it back.'

'Don't be a pillock all your life – take a day off. It wasn't Farouk.'

'Well Farouk was king wan he?'

'It was Nasser who started it by taking control.'

'Well okay, whoever it was he had good reason to, the Yanks broke a promise that they would help put up the dough so's he could build a dam – the Coolie Dam it was for the Gyppo's.'

'It wasn't the Coolie Dam, you berk, it was the Aswan Dam and the reason the Yanks broke their promise is that Nasser had gone over to the commies in Russia.'

'No he hadn't.'

'Yes he had.'

'He hadn't.'

'He had, I tell you. Be told.'

'Bollocks!'

The debate dried up with yawns and rough g'nights.

The London Docks: Working By

'D'you mind working by for a spell?' It was a question that received a varied response from whomever it was asked of. If you were full of spit and vinegar it fell on deaf ears because you'd want to get away to Rio or maybe Shanghai. For a man who'd been about a bit, however, perhaps in his thirties and trying to repair or maintain a relationship with his wife and children, then the question might get a positive response. 'No, not at all,' might be his reply, thus earning himself brownie points both at home and in the shipping office.

The dockside, crammed with vessels tied up bow to stern, needed temporary crew to man them until those who were returning for another voyage were back from leave: not a full crew but enough within the catering department to cover shore-side requirements. Leading hands and officers, who stayed aboard overnight, would still expect their breakfasts and their cabins made up each morning. Apart from the unloading and loading of general cargo, shore-side personnel and numerous visitors were all over the ship for a multiplicity of reasons. Engineers were below, calibrating and replacing gauges and ancillary equipment, perhaps fitting in new boiler-feed controls before the next voyage.

There'd be supplements to stores for all departments arriving daily. Customs and Excise might have a rummage crew aboard, with eager young recruits in training, seeking out hidden baccy or booze. Although all such personnel were not entitled to lunch in the dining saloon, many turned up to try it on. As a table steward once you'd sussed the meal situation out you could earn quite well; a nod and a wink from those who didn't want their credentials questioned too closely before you fed them at your table, and your tips could be more than your daily pay.

I did quite a few stints of 'working by' but only on a ship that I intended to sail on. It could be a sweet little number for a steward, whether he slept on board or went home to the missus and the family, because by about 1500 hours his duties for the day were over and he could be home in time to watch *'Noggin the Nog'* with the kiddy. Some hardly ever went to sea, had really gotten into the lifestyle and been doing so for years. As they were legitimately still in the service, conscription couldn't get them and it could be a great life; down the Round House every night or up in Canning Town at the Bridge House. Those who did go home could watch *'Juke Box Jury'* or *'Quatermass'* on their newly acquired telly and could be tucked up with the wife by half past ten.

The experiences of working by a ship were many and would be related and embellished into yarns in the stewards' mess when you were back at sea. Such tales could raise a laugh and an eyebrow or two...

'So where was I? Oh yeah, this bloke says to the Headwaiter, "You got a minute, chief? We're looking for someone in charge like." But no, the Headwaiter hasn't got a minute and why? Because he only came aboard that morning and is right up the wall. The Chief and Second Steward are both still on leave, all the wingers have buggered off and he's got to get the saloon linen bagged up and ashore for the laundry by four.

"Can you help, chief? We're up in the lounge on B deck and we've come about the piano, it'll only take a second to explain. If we leave it any later you won't have it back before you sail."

He's a dapper looking bloke in a bow tie and tweeds and he seems earnest enough to anticipate any problems that could arise. So anyway, minutes later, they're all up in the observation lounge on B deck; the dapper bloke has the lid of the grand piano open and is tinkling the ivories up and down the scales. But with a sad look on his face, he shakes his head. "No, pity really, it's gonna have to go away. If we could have done it here it would have saved the company a lot of trouble and expense. The hammers have gone, see! You'll want a receipt of course. Those concertina doors out onto the deck, chief; can we have them open and I'll get the crane-man to swing it? We've got all the gear, Harold go and..." And it's the last anyone sees of the Bechstein grand piano.'

**

The Royal group of docks comprised the Royal Albert, King George V and Victoria Docks. Situated opposite Woolwich and parallel to the river on the northern bank of the Thames, they were built between 1880 and 1921 and were the largest enclosed docks in the world. The area totalled 1,100 acres, which might be difficult to visualize but they were equivalent in size to the whole of central London from Hyde Park to Tower Bridge. That was only the Royal group. Add to that the West India Docks, sometimes known as Poplar Docks and The Pool of London and you had enough moorings to float a few boats.

But then again that was only on the northern bank of the Thames. Located on the Rotherhithe peninsula farther west on the South Bank were the Surrey Docks, and it was here that *The Mayflower* called before taking on more crew and setting out from Harwich in 1620, to visit Plymouth and arguably embarking additional Pilgrim Fathers for the New World.

Just upstream at Deptford was where Henry the Eighth had his Royal Naval Dockyard. Resident at Greenwich Palace, almost next door, Henry could nip round to keep an eye on them, get away from whatever missus was giving him grief and maybe have a sly grog now and then with the lads.

Being a seaman, therefore, and setting off on various voyages it wasn't difficult with hindsight to feel part of a tradition. I say with hindsight because there would not have been many seamen at the time, myself included, who would have been aware of such historical facts.

Going 'down to the docks' then wasn't exactly a precise location and you needed advice about what train or bus to catch: never mind travelling the world but where do I get off, is it Plaistow or East Ham?

Working by on the London docks could also come close to living dangerously, particularly for those who didn't have a home to go to, had only the vessel to stay on or the Flying Angel seamen's mission to lodge in. For company a man tended to go ashore of an evening with those he worked by with. In itself this was a good thing because socializing with the lads you were working with made the job more fun and an easy-going attitude prevailed.

'Coming ashore?' could sometimes be a loaded question from a bloke that you might have only met an hour or two earlier. But recklessly ignoring a cautionary vibe you'd hear yourself reply, 'Yeah, let's go sailor,' and that could result in getting into a situation beyond your control. You both might, after a skin-full, find yourself in a Squaddies' pub, like The Ordnance Arms over the river in Woolwich, just opposite the Arsenal, only to realize that 'Sailor boy' had a thing about khaki and for some reason hated those who wore it. It wasn't long before his behaviour and loud insults toward the battalion had set you both out on a predetermined path.

Full of Dutch courage by now and giving 'back up' to your newfound mate, you might not wish to appear frightened of a little spilt claret so finding yourself drawn into a discussion that was becoming heated with a soldier about his parentage, you might have missed Sailor boy (who's now standing on a table) giving out a verbal challenge...

'We're the Merch and can take on any lousy squaddies who're up for it.' It could prove to be an interesting and partially memorable evening and it would only be later and in retrospect, perhaps after expensive dental work or when the plaster came off, that you could reflect on the mistakes you had made by going ashore with a complete and utter nutter.

Going ashore on your own wasn't risk free either. Skiddering down the slippery spiral steps of the Woolwich foot tunnel could have its moments and subsequent horrors as I well remember. Late on a freezing winter's night with snow upon the ground, and having had too many winter warmers of barley wine and those jellied eels bought earlier from Tubby Isaacs, I did just that. My destination was a cosy bunk back aboard the ship within the Royal Albert Docks, but barley wine and the spiral steps descending into the tunnel, going round and round, can have a delayed affect.

It might have been just as I was about half way through, beneath the river, that I felt the need to stop to rest my aching head against the cool tiles of the tunnel wall. It might have only been a minute or two but deciding to continue I realized I'd lost my bearings; the tunnel stretched into what appeared infinity in both directions and there was no one down there to ask, or even a sign. The Authority, maybe the PLA or Woolwich Council, had blithely assumed that whoever went into the tunnel knew what direction they were going, and a sign wasn't needed. I set off again uncertainly but shortly came to graffiti scrawled in crayon upon the tunnel wall by some helpful soul, which confirmed that I was going in the right direction. It said, **'YOU ARE HERE! KEEP GOING.'** Sure enough after another fifteen minutes and climbing the steps I emerged back from whence I'd started, back in Woolwich on the south side. It's a problem that you never encounter when travelling across on the ferry but they had of course stopped for the night. The foot tunnel is open 24/7 and was the only way to cross to North Woolwich, so I set off again tired but wiser, eventually emerging, and hoping I was in time for the last bus. There were many mistakes that night and I wasn't finished with them either.

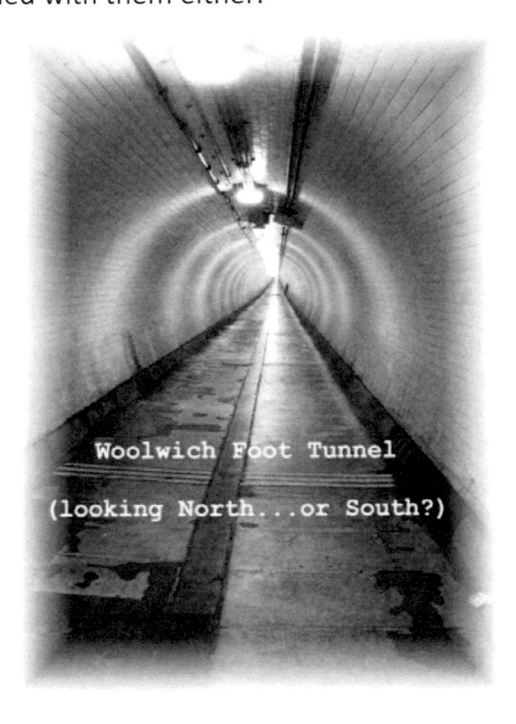

Woolwich Foot Tunnel (looking North...or South?)

Successfully catching the last 101 bus towards East Ham could be considered another one. I swung myself aboard and went up the stairs into a smoky interior. Throwing myself into the first available seat I closed my eyes and tried to still my revolving head as the bus turned right and left, but no I was aware of becoming more, not less, giddy. First my mouth went dry then it became too wet, as pressure began somewhere below, thus warning me that the jellied eels might be planning to make a comeback. I opened my eyes and tried to focus. Less than twelve inches in front of me was the back of a man's bald head in animated conversation with a woman sitting beside it. Below that his crimson neck bulged obscenely over a collar.

'All fares please!' said the jovial conductor standing beside me, now blocking any potential escape. From then on my recall of events became confused but everything was later to replay itself in slow motion: the tsunami of semi-digested jellied eels and barley wine bathing the man's bald head, his outrage, the disgust apparent on the conductor's features, the shouts and cries, the rude language, the escalation of voice and violence as I was hauled from my seat by strong arms and propelled backwards down the stairs. Then from the swaying platform of the moving vehicle I was ejected off it into the night... the soft, white, blessed snow... the tail-lights of the disappearing bus.

Perhaps there were too many mistakes that winter's night but attempting to comfort myself later I remembered my father's voice from many years ago. It was something he had often said, perhaps to console his Irish soul in similar situations: 'Sure to God! Wasn't it your man who never made a mistake who never made anything?'

A One-Way Trip

It was to be during January of the New Year, 1961 when an opportunity presented itself that would open up a new chapter in my life. I was aboard the Shaw Savill cargo passenger vessel *Ceramic* returning from New Zealand and working in the dining saloon as a winger. The ship was due to call at Pitcairn Island within a day or two and interest aboard regarding the mutiny on the *Bounty* was running high. Lunch was almost over and I had served coffee to those on my table who were discussing the affair.

One of my passengers, Captain Gerry Theakston, travelling with his wife, seemed quite knowledgeable about Captain Bligh, and the others around the table were listening politely. I was listening with half an ear whilst busy refilling the salt and pepper cellars on my dummy. Tahiti was mentioned and Captain Theakston volunteered the information that he would be calling there during the following April on his return to New Zealand, which gave rise to questions as to why.

'Gerry is delivering a ship to Auckland, aren't you dear, and it's a port of call for us,' said Mrs Theakston. My half an ear toward the conversation very rapidly became a full ear and in my excitement I overfilled the salt cellar, spilling salt all over my dummy. Blimey! If Captain Theakston was going to deliver a ship to New Zealand then he'd want a crew, wouldn't he? And it would have to be a one-way crew. Wow! Make your mind up time, Joe!

In January 1961 I was 23 and had no real idea of what I wanted to do with my life. Fully aware of my lack of a proper education and any decent qualifications, I was prepared to drift along satisfying my curiosity about the world with a vague idea that one day something would turn up. I had no real aspirations and certainly never thought of myself as being clever enough to attempt anything like a career. I knew I didn't want to be a waiter all my life, or even to remain in Catering, but what else to do? I just knew that what I'd overheard could have some significance for my future.

With Mrs Theakston's explanation to the table, my future became somehow more tangible. Perhaps a new life for me could begin in Christchurch, where Mum and Rosie had relocated. Suddenly everything seemed filled with promise, and I became anxious to know if Captain Theakston could offer me a one-way trip.

The following morning, after breakfast, I had a moment to request a quiet word with him and explained my interest. The result was that yes, he would be requiring a crew and yes there could be a place for me on the delivery ship, the *John Wilson*, as a steward. Simple as that! I was ecstatic.

New Zealand had such appeal to those seamen who had visited there that many had jumped ship to live and work there. Sometimes it would be on impulse, usually with a woman involved. Others planned it more methodically, perhaps jumping in Australia and travelling or 'ring-bolting' to New Zealand, whereby they could claim they had arrived legitimately. Either way residency could prove difficult and often involved eventually being caught or handing themselves over to the authorities, whereby they might serve a short time in prison and then be repatriated to their mother country. But by then they had made a decision to stay, become a daddy or had earned enough by working hard in a variety of jobs, so had saved the necessary fare and could enter the country legitimately.

The plan, as Captain Theakston explained to me, was for me to stay ashore in the UK until March or possibly early April. We exchanged contact details and he said he would send me a telegram when it was time join the ship, a bulk cement carrier in Grangemouth. The ship required commissioning and then sea trials on the Forth and for that I would be needed. I was over the moon about the whole idea and the more I thought about it the more I became convinced that it was right for me. I paid off the *Ceramic,* took temporary employment ashore as a factory hand with Glaxo Laboratories in Uxbridge and lodged with Dave Symes, who had left the sea, married his girlfriend, started a family and was living in Hillingdon. Neat!

The Captain was as good as his word and I received a telegram and a travel voucher to join the ship in April. Quite why it was named *John Wilson* I have no idea, but was this to be a glimpse into the future? I had my own cabin and there existed a much more relaxed attitude aboard between officers and crew.

Or maybe my new skipper, being a relatively young man himself and having experience of working on New Zealand-owned ships, was not to be stifled by the outdated British ideas of class and hierarchy that hitherto had been my experience. It was a small vessel and a happy one. We called at the usual ports: Curaçao, Balboa, Pitcairn Island but also, as mentioned in an earlier chapter, we called in at Tahiti where we berthed in Papeete alongside a replica of the *Bounty*.

There were no madcap runs ashore as in the past, and all crew seemed to be on their most gentlemanly behaviour. Maybe they were hoping to stay with the vessel on the Kiwi coast, or like me, had a purpose and were ready for a new chapter in their lives.

I do remember that we stayed there longer than originally intended and whether that was because the island had its own magical charm and beauty or because we had a young skipper, I'm uncertain. Or could it have been that one of the engineers jumped ship, believing he had arrived in paradise and we had to find a replacement?

The women were beautiful but dignified and with leis around their necks would dance hulas for us. If we did buy them a drink, they'd buy us one back. I also remember several of the crew having their photos taken with a large man who seemed to have made a living out of his reputedly being Paul Gauguin's son. Several weeks at sea, with my own cabin and not being overburdened with work, allowed me time to get my head on straight and to think seriously about some sort of future shore-side. What would I do? What could I do? I didn't realise it at the time but with hindsight again (great thing, hindsight) I might have been preparing myself to remove the badge that had been pinned to me on leaving school, ten years earlier, which proclaimed I was fit only for menial work and had hitherto caused me to suffer from a lack of aspiration.

We arrived in Auckland on the 15th May 1961, and I was asked to stay aboard until a replacement steward was found. This I did, eventually flying down to Christchurch several days later to meet Mum and Rosie, who were waiting for me at Christchurch airport. It was so good to see them and to be home and living with them again. There were items from our past that I'd forgotten all about: the old mantle clock in its place above the grate and behind which we'd kept receipts and paid bills, crockery and cutlery from childhood, even our old curtains – patterned with flowers – that Mum had saved up for and bought to hang in the front room of our new council house all those years ago.

They'd all been in storage somewhere, waiting until Mum had found somewhere to live independently of her employer. She and Rosie had stayed with Mr Coleman for nearly three years but the isolation of the hill country had eventually got them down, and it wasn't fair on my sister. They had then moved to the South Island where they both found employment and accommodation at Lincoln College, just a bus ride from Christchurch. But now they were renting a three-bedroom bungalow in Cashel Street, Mum working in a department store and Rosie as seamstress for a small outfit nearby.

Peter Joseph Troy

A Respectable Job

I had to wear a tie but they supplied the brown coat. The telephone was ringing and I knew how to answer it. 'Stockroom,' I said, and then listened to the request. 'Two ticks please,' and I repeated the request to Pat, my new boss. 'Have we a copy of Cobban's *History of Modern France*, volume two?' 'Re-printing,' Pat replied. 'Not available till November.'

I gave the caller the answer and hung up. Pat seemed to have a photographic memory for all books and within my first week I had grown to like and respect him. In his thirties, he had no dress sense, spoke a bit posh and always had a fag on. With fag ash on his waistcoat, he took his lunch break in the stockroom, seated in a canvas-folding chair, with a flask of tea, sandwiches and usually a thick book that he seemed to be absorbed in.

I'd seen the job advertised only the previous week, gone into Whitcombe's and had been offered it to start the following Monday. I really liked helping to unpack the large cartons full of books that had arrived from abroad and tick off the invoices. Part of my job was to barrow in the books to the Education

Department where staff would put them on the relevant shelves. I was getting to know people and they were getting to know me. There was Sylvie, who seemed to know as much as Pat about stock and was very confident serving customers and operating the till. A bloke about my age called Lindsay was friendly and lived with his folks in Fendalton. I was beginning to fit in and felt good about my ability to pick up what was required of me. I kept quiet about my background as I had given myself two GCE's on the application form and hoped I wouldn't be questioned too closely about qualifications.

I was now a legitimate New Zealand citizen and it felt right. Sir Iain Ferguson had become the Governor General and Mr Holyoake, leader of the National Party, was Prime Minister and also the Minister for Foreign Affairs. His reluctance to send troops to the Vietnam War that had begun two years earlier caused disagreement with ANZUS, which had been formed during WW II. He was no doubt reminded by the other two members that NZ now had a greater responsibility toward its US and Australian allies than toward the Mother Country. As a result there were to be protests and marches over the possibility of New Zealanders being sent to fight in what would be a controversial conflict. Greater changes were ahead for NZ as Britain was negotiating for stronger Common Market ties, and Mr Heath's input was viewed with growing alarm by those New Zealanders who had hitherto relied heavily on their exports to the UK. The old idea of Commonwealth was in a state of flux beginning perhaps with India's independence in 1947 and later, Britain's loss of Suez.

Canterbury mornings were cold, often with a frost, but by midday the sun shone strong from out of a clear blue sky and I loved it. The seasons were of course reversed and by September spring was on its way, the daffodils beginning to show in Hagley Park. A new school term was nearly on us; the Education Department of Whitcombe & Tombs was gearing up for a busy time and I had been asked to help occasionally behind the counter in the shop. I felt a bit scared about handling the till and giving change, but Mum helped me over that hurdle by playing 'shop and till work' over the kitchen table after tea. With a ten bob note she'd 'buy a book for three and six' and I'd count out the change into her hand. I soon got the hang of it all and began to enjoy my newfound skills of serving customers and operating the till.

'Cobban's *History of Modern France* Sir? We have part one but part two won't be available until next month. Would you like me to reserve a copy for you?' The words were spilling from my lips and listening to myself, I marvelled at my newfound erudition.

My earlier skills as a steward, knowing how to talk to and wait on passengers, served me well in my newfound role and I became good at my job. When within a few months a position became available at Whitcombe's 'University Bookshop', almost on campus at the University of Canterbury, I applied and was accepted. Don was the manager, calm and relaxed in his efficiency, and he became my perfect mentor. Apart from two part-timers, Roger and Heidi, and an occasional student to help out, I was the only other full-timer. I discovered that I had a natural aptitude for the work. A memory for titles, authors and publishers, even though I knew nothing of what lay within the covers of such academic books, permitted me to become a source of information to visiting academic staff, and I began to lose my sycophantic manner when talking to them.

The majority of textbooks were of course imported from Europe or the USA; therefore anything required had to be ordered weeks and months ahead from a variety of publishers. The academic staff of course knew this and liaison between them and us, their suppliers at Whitcombe & Tombs, became important if textbooks and recommended reading were to be available for students at the start of term and throughout the academic year. Professor Lodgekin, Head of the Russian Department and a shambling bear of a man, would call in with a list of titles to be ordered from the publishing house Novy Mir in Moscow, perhaps written in both Russian and English. These would have to be correctly copied out by me on the ordering form. I can't remember making a mistake; the Prof got his books and I got his approval.

Within a few months Don decided to leave to do a fulltime Masters degree (in Anthropology if I remember right), so I became the acting manager and began to fire on all cylinders. Each person coming into the bookshop with a request for a book I took on as a challenge to see if I would have the answer in my head.

'Cotton's *Principles of Electrical Technology*?' Certainly, Sir, should be here on the shelf...Yep here we are, latest edition, three pound seventeen and sixpence'.

'Margaret Mead's *Coming of Age in Samoa*? Would you like the paperback or the bound edition? We have both.'

'Theatre of the Absurd? No, sorry should be in end of the month but yes we have Pinter's *'Birthday Party'*. That to a keen young student called James Laurenson, who would later become well known as a Shakespearean actor on the London Stage.

I had the keys to the shop and for about twelve months it felt as though I had the keys to the City. I rose to the responsibility of my role, but despite it being a white-collar job the pay was low. I knew I was good at what I had to do but still felt I was 'winging it'. Then after a while the job became tame. I missed the camaraderie of those who'd been my buddies for the past several years and although at first I seemed to fit in with my bookish colleagues, the tie around my neck was just too tight. It's true that you can take a man from the sea and his mates, but can you take the sea and his mates from the man?

I needed friends, but more importantly I was impatient for romance and that wasn't even on the horizon. At that time Christchurch was the world centre of the early night, and the last bus from Cathedral Square left at half past nine. I took books home with me and got my head around commercial arithmetic and algebra; there wasn't a lot else to do, certainly no TV, which thinking back on it was a blessing. But after about two years I knew the dream was fading for me. When I was down I was a submerged submarine, lurking, yet out of sight. Up would come the old periscope above the surface from time to time, rotate through 360 degrees on the lookout for a pair of lips to kiss, or a pair of tits to nuzzle. Sex had become a memory and I was anxious to let go my torpedoes; to score a direct hit and see my objective erupt into noise and orgasmic flame.

Not a submarine but a car? Yep, that was the answer. Get a pair of wheels and the tits would fall into my soft but greedy palms. My old buddy Johnny Murray, now living in Wellington, had his own window cleaning business, was growing rich, had loads of friends and the women were willing. Others I had sailed with were working on the waterfront, all of them wearing blue collars but earning really well. I felt the tug to go and join them but before I did, why not buy a car and give Christchurch another chance but maybe with a different job?

The Black & the Chrome

Psychologist's claim that the type of car we choose indicates a lot about our personality. Maybe they're right, and I started out with modest ideas about the model. Yeah, an Austin A40 would do...mmm I'd think about it. The motors shimmering on Harry's used car lot looked penned in as they sweltered in the summer sun. They needed to be let out onto the open road with their windows down, and I was tempted to get off the morning bus to work and drive them all out to the Cashmere Hills, bringing them back under a starlit sky. I would look up from my Raymond Chandler paperback and gaze wistfully at what was on daily display. Beneath the bunting, the advertising and the balloons were Austins, Rileys, Wolseys and Hillmans baking in the alien heat. With their dashboards of maple veneer and smelling of rich leather these British imports never seemed to really belong. Not even here in this most English of New Zealand cities. They were too indigenous to their native landscape to have been loaded onto steamers and banished 12,000 miles from their mother country. Where once they had gracefully rolled and beeped along English country lanes, or featured in poems by John Betjeman, they now seemed tired and defeated – as in some foreign field.

Their primness set them apart from their brash American cousins: the Chryslers and Dodges, the Studebakers and Oldsmobiles that loitered carelessly about, full of jive and jazz, on the other side of Harry's lot. These Damn Yankees were as much at home here on the Canterbury plains as they ever were in the streets of Chicago or on the desert roads of the American Midwest.

'She's a bonzer motor – a lovely runner.' Harry had waddled up in shirtsleeves and braces. Through the open window of his little sales shed the radio blared. Helen Shapiro was *'Walking back to happiness; yeah-heh! Oh yea heh - heh...*! I gently kicked a whitewall tyre and tried not to look too captivated as Harry stood beside me, both of us lost in admiration of the '52 Chevy. It wasn't late but night came down early at this latitude. Harry's car lot was lit by powerful beams from above, and strings of coloured bulbs and red and green neons flashing on and off gave the place a fairground effect.

1952 CHEVROLET STYLELINE DELUXE 4-DOOR SEDAN

'Take her for a spin whenever you like, sport,' said Harry shooting me a conspiratorial grin. My mouth went dry and I stuttered something about 'just looking'.

Friday night, this particular one humid with spatterings of warm rain that came and went in brief showers carrying with them wafts of tropical vegetation, was New Zealand's traditional late night shopping time and the town was busy. Sheep farmers with their wives and families had driven in many miles from across the plains to take advantage, perhaps to take in a movie, buy a milkshake or Mum some new curtains.

With a pudgy finger Harry flicked the ticket on the windscreen. 'At this price though she'll be snapped up pretty damn quick.' I tried to look laid back but the notion that some farmer would buy the Chevrolet and maybe fill it with sheep caused my brain to go into overdrive. I took a swallow. 'Jump in, sit behind the wheel, get the feel of her,' said Harry.

'Get the feel of her!' There it was, the seduction. I got a twitch from down there and luckily just then Harry's attention was taken by two jokers in cow-cocky hats who were opening the door of a blue Ford Consul several motors away. 'Well give us a shout if you want the keys,' he called out cheerfully as he sailed off toward them. I breathed out slowly and took a stroll around the beast.

'Her?' This was no 'her'. Beaded with a million tiny raindrops, its waxed and polished surfaces of black and chrome glistened in the lighting and neons. *Say goodbye to lone-li-ness.* The song and the night full of warm promise seemed to conspire with the automobile. Its streamlined sleekiness throbbed with latent power – patient but ready. If it came to anything at all, if this was the start of a relationship then I'd have to be clear about who would be the driver and who, the driven.

I tried the door, it was open. As I smoothly slid in behind the wheel and dashboard I felt myself wrapped about in a Phillip Marlow trench coat with its collar upturned and a snap-brim fedora on my head. I reached for my ivory cigarette case – a present from Big Al. With a Lucky Strike between my lips I snapped my fingers, and Louie beside me reached across with a light. Winding down the window I breathed out a pale wreath of blue smoke into the warm aromatic night. If that fink Harry came around again I'd get Louie to slap him around some. In the driving mirror I caught a movement. It was a dame in the back seat, blonde hair over one eye. She was smouldering, giving me the big come-on, anxious to be in the Cashmere Hills with me. Well she'd have to wait, wait till I was good and ready for her.

I took in the layout of the interior. Clever design had moved the gear lever from the floor to the steering column: an engineering triumph of lascivious intent, it allowed the seating to run unbroken the width of the vehicle. I smiled to myself and took another drag on my Lucky. American know-how had removed what had been an effective deterrent to any shenanigans that I might get up to – and that was only the front seat. What lay in the back with Veronica, once I told Louie to take a powder, was going to be a very private investigation, or I was no Dick. My future seemed assured, so I made up my mind right there and then. Next week I would learn to drive.

Winging It

Peter Harrison was a Pom and an ex-seaman, who worked as a waiter in a restaurant in New Brighton. Quite how we met evades me but when we did we found we both spoke the same language. We joined a martial arts group where we began to learn judo, and also went to The United Services Hotel where he taught me to drink Bacardi. We found out that Christchurch actually had a night club called The Plainsman, located above a furniture shop. Okay, so they only sold coffee or orange juice but we brown–bagged it with small bottles of Bacardi and sly-grogged it with the orange juice. Chubby Checker was all the rage and everyone was twisting the night away – right through the small hours till about half past ten when they closed for the night.

Pete had a pal who worked for Electrolux as a door to door salesman. The wage was low but the commission was high for every vacuum cleaner sold, and this pal was making big money. I needed big money if I was to ever get that Chevy, so we both of us went for an interview, got offered the chance to join the company and immediately packed in our current jobs. From one point of view this was a retrograde step for me but by then I was looking for the main chance, and I had never been the prudent type. We had two weeks in the company's classroom learning all about the product and developing our sales technique before we were taken out by the Sales Manager, Mr Skelly, to knock on a few doors. Owning a car would be the ideal and something to give us a motive to sell as many vacuum cleaners as possible, thus earning fat commissions. Until that time we would go out in groups of three or four with a salesman who had a car, out to the suburbs of the city. We would of course all pitch in with cash for the petrol.

Mr Skelly, mid-forties, horn-rimmed glasses, broad shouldered and barrel-chested, is walking up the garden path of a respectable semi in the suburb of Wainoni. It's early 1963, a hot morning and the sun blazes down. Mr Skelly is showing us how it's done. Peter Harrison and I are across the street, sitting in the back of his black Opel car with the windows down, observing. He knocks loudly on the front door and then wanders several yards back down the path towards the gate, where he crouches and appears to be studying a bedding plant. Meanwhile the front door opens a crack and then opens wider as the housewife looks out, shielding her eyes from the brightness of the morning. Skelly seems not to have noticed so she steps out to enquire, 'Good morning?' Skelly then stands up. 'Oh, Good morning,' he smiles, 'I was just admiring your flowers.'

He knows sod-all about plants but his tactic now has the housewife over her doorstep with the door wide open and he's ready with the spiel. 'We're in the area this week, from Electrolux,' he says moving slowly toward her. She is shaking her head. 'Oh no thank you, we already have one.'

'Yes,' says Skelly unperturbed [Always crown the prospect's 'no' with a 'yes'], 'we have you in our records and that's why we're here. We're offering a free maintenance check and filter replacement this month; just part of our after sales service. Is it okay to check now or should I make an appointment to come back next year?' [Give 'em a choice] She doesn't want to miss out on the freebie but she's still not sure. Skelly seems to produce a clipboard from nowhere and checks an item on it. 'Should take no more than five minutes,' he says and he appears so confident that she'll allow him in that she does. After he follows her across the threshold, Pete and I get out of the car and open the boot. It's worked before and we know it's about to work again.

Sure enough, after three or four minutes have ticked by Skelly appears at the open door and nods his head. Pete has a set of filters in his hand and both of us set out across the street, leaving the boot open. It is, after all, 1963 and this is Wainoni, where 'opportunity crime' is unheard of. When we enter Skelly introduces us to Mrs Taylor and explains that we are technicians in training. [No mention of sales] By now he has his jacket off and is in shirtsleeves and braces. We all look like bank managers or hit-men: stiff double-breasted suits, collars and ties and highly polished shoes. Skelly is crouched again, this time over a mid-fifties bottle-green Electrolux vacuum cleaner. We recognize it as the C41 model, it's plugged in and he's turning it on and off with his hand held intermittently over the air intake. Head cocked to one side he's listening to the bearings.

'Very good suction,' he says and Mrs Taylor smiles and nods agreement. She seems to make up her mind and kindly asks if we would like a cool drink. 'Is lemon squash all right?' she asks.

We are all very grateful and murmur our thanks. By the time she is back Pete and I have removed our coats, too, and everything seems informal.

'Mr Harrison,' says Skelly - looking at Pete. 'With Mrs Taylor's permission I would like to conduct a quick comparative test with the new prototype, but only if that is all right?' He smiles at her and how can she refuse – how often does she get visitors like us out here in the boondocks?

'Should take only another five minutes and it will give Mrs Taylor a chance to see the future,' he says. Pete knows the score and is across the street in a flash, lifting a large oblong cardboard box out of the boot. When he gets back I'm on my knees, removing the filter from the rear of the C41. It's filthy and I'm getting a few coughs out as I leave it on display on her smart carpeting. I take a long draught of my cool drink and Mrs Taylor is looking apologetic, if not a little ashamed, at the state of her filter – it's obvious it has never been cleaned: thick grey congealed dust and what looks like dog hairs interwoven into it. I show her the new filter, pristine and white, before putting it into her old machine. Skelly picks up the old filter as if it's a dog-turd, holding it at arm's length and pops it into the plastic bag from whence the new one has emerged; it is an awkward moment but designed to be so. Skelly praises her C41, telling Pete and me that it was the best model Electrolux ever produced before the new technology came in. We nod our agreement, docile and in deference to his encyclopaedic knowledge of such things.

There is something of the games-show host about Skelly, which those residents who were lucky enough to have a black and white television and reasonable reception might have

Below Decks

recognized: he looks a bit like Melvin Toogood, a sort of cross between Clark Kent and the Incredible Hulk. In a flash of chrome extension tubes and with a standard nozzle attached, he proceeds to quickly mantle up Mrs Taylor's C41 and is energetically vacuuming the main carpet. We all take a step back giving him room in which to demonstrate his mastery of the art. To see a meaty man like Skelly wielding the C41 seems surreal; he looks as if he'd be more at home with a grenade launcher and appears as miscast as say Jack Palance would be auditioning for the role of Elizabeth Bennet. He speaks up above the loud hum, repeating his earlier comment about the suction but draws our attention to the noisy state of the bearings. He gives the carpet a good going over, back and forth, then at right angles. He goes at it with such gusto that I wonder if the pattern in the carpet is going to resist his efforts. He turns the C41 off and not until the bearings have rattled into silence does he say anything more.

'Very, very good machine, the C41,' he says. 'You won't need to replace the bearings for at least another year, Mrs Taylor.' [Damning with faint praise]

'Mr Troy?' He nods at me and already I'm unplugging her C41, wrapping it up and putting it out of sight, and Pete has the new machine, the Z01, out of the box. The Z01 has not been on display, the punters will not have found it in any shop and it has not been advertised, so its sudden appearance in Mrs Taylor's front room — all cream plastic and pink streamlining, light weight and with futuristic lines — is guaranteed to knock socks off. It really is the future and Mrs Taylor's eyes have widened; quite what other physiological changes have taken place within her anatomy is not hinted at in 1963. There exists a hushed silence but already we can feel, if not hear, the first strains of *'Thus*

Spake Zarathustra' vibrating through Mrs Taylor's frame and arteries. At this point we know we could all drop our pants and moon at her and she wouldn't notice; but of course we don't, not wishing to break the spell under which she now, trance-like, is gazing at the new machine.

Pete's getting into the swing of demonstrating this machine, having done it about a 242 times in the company's classroom. He takes out the polished aluminium extension tubes, removes the tissue paper covering and passes one over to Mrs Taylor.

'Notice how light they are,' he tells her as she takes it. 'Much lighter than your old chrome tubes. Most people think they're aluminium but they are actually a much lighter alloy, developed for the Space Project at NASA.'

Skelly, having done his bit, sits back in an armchair and lights up a thin cigarillo; an expert would recognize the subtle shifting of influence and control within the room. Skelly's body language is testimony to the fact that he has done this a million times and knows whatever liberty he may be taking is just not noticed by Mrs Taylor. Had it been someone less experienced they might have asked permission to sit or to light up, but to do so would have ruptured such a hypnotic moment. He could probably cop a feel and she wouldn't mind.

Pete has everything plugged in and the new machine is ready for action but he does not turn it on; I have moved the new box and packing and there is just Pete, Mrs Taylor and the pattern in the carpet. A faint low hum now fills the room as Pete turns the machine on and a small red neon lights up as he passes the connected tube to Mrs Taylor, suggesting she may like to try it out. Her old C41 doesn't have castors – only sled-type runners –

but this new sleek beauty does, and it follows her around like a faithful pup. She is so into the ease of it all that Pete and I sit down too. After she has finished the carpet she's out into the hall and Pete waits till he hears her on the stairs before he selects the stair attachment and crevice nozzle. After he's given her more spiel he leaves her to it. [You can oversell a product] He comes back in and we all sit quietly – taking a load off – and can hear her doing the landing now. Pete's getting the paperwork and carbon paper ready on her small coffee table, but keeps it out of sight.

When she comes back into the front room all bright eyed and excited, we all stand up, gentlemen that we are. A comparative test involves checking just what the machine has picked up so Skelly asks for an old newspaper. We all appear gob-smacked at just how much dust comes out of the dust-bag [Ugh!].

No one so far has mentioned the idea of selling her the new machine and we're packing things away and putting on our coats. It's at this point she seems to come to and asks what price does the Z01 retail at, but quickly adds that she certainly is not interested at the moment in buying a new one. Skelly now tells Mrs Taylor that the new machine is not yet on sale in the South Island and how desperate his wife is for one. He mentions import quotas for household appliances manufactured abroad and goes on about how unfair he thinks it is that only those in the capital - Wellington - can buy such a machine. At this point Peter Harrison takes his cue and speaks up.

'I was in the office quite early this morning, Mr Skelly, and Mr Wilson told me that we were in fact expecting a delivery later today.' Skelly seems stunned by such news but having been away with Mrs Skelly for the past week on a trip to the west coast... well a week can be a long time and anyway, he reminds us there is a waiting list for those who are eager for the Z01.

'Mrs Taylor, would you mind if I use your phone to ring the office?' he asks politely. 'Just to check if there is anything available.' Just to check to be sure you've won the Golden Kiwi, he could have said, going by the way she is all agreement. The phone call goes on for a bit and yes it is confirmed that a delivery is expected later today but only for fifteen machines. Skelly is relaying this info to us all in Mrs Taylor's front room with his big mitt holding the phone; which means that we do have five Z01s for sale after we have taken care of those on the waiting list. Pete and I are over the moon with such good news and are beaming at Mrs Taylor, who is beaming back.

Pete gets the commission from this sale but I get Mrs Taylor's old C41 that we'd allowed her in part exchange. It's worth about a fiver to me from a bloke I'd got to know. Skelly will get a beer out of it but the retainer that he's on to train his 'technicians' up more than compensates. Mrs Skelly? Well she's got her eye on the new Z02 and it really is something else. It comes with a hair-drying attachment and paint-spraying device. I mean you really have to see the new technology...

Despite the training I found I didn't have what it took to sell door to door, unlike some of the blokes. A hungry Aussie did really well and often came top of the team but he was ruthless: 'They've got my dough and I'm gonna get it,' he'd say – and he did. Pete Harrison went out with him to see what he was doing right and we weren't. Pete realized then that Oz was in a different league when he watched his technique. He would get over the threshold easily with the filter story but then his actions became unethical, as well as highly dramatic.

Out would come the housewife's vacuum cleaner from beneath the stairs, and Oz would plug it in and appear to receive a small shock through the tips of his fingers, enough to ask, 'How long has it been like this?' Then warning anyone within the vicinity not to touch it, he would produce a voltmeter and a pair of rubber gloves from his briefcase. With the range set low to measure resistance the needle would go off scale and register an alarming reading.

'Jesus Christ,' he'd say jumping back and quickly unplugging the machine from the mains. 'Don't touch it, it's live!' He would then appear to recover himself and apologize for taking the Lord's name in vain. If Oz knew he could get away with it, he'd go back to his car and reappear wearing a crash helmet, forbidding the housewife to ever use her vacuum cleaner again and enquiring if children ever came near it. No wonder he was top of the team. Pete and I, despite our youth, had scruples and were not that hard-nosed, so we didn't earn like some of the guys did.

Within a short time Pete met Colleen, a pretty nurse, at the Plainsman, fell in love, married her, and they both took off to Auckland. I was either best man at the wedding or I gave the bride away...*Oh yes I remember it well.* They had little money so it was a budget do: no photographer in attendance and no car. After the formalities at the church we all got a bus into Christchurch, Colleen in her bridal wear complete with veil and bouquet, and went to the photographer's studio for about two or three shots to remember the occasion by.

I wasn't to see Pete for several years and when I did, they had by then produced a lovely child, Paula. They remained married until 2009 when sadly Colleen departed this life.

Back to Windy Wellington

In November of 1963 I moved up to Wellington, found digs and took a job, any job, out at a factory in Upper Hutt. I was back, blue-collar again after two-and-a-half years in Christchurch, and it felt good not having to wear a tie. Most people of my generation or thereabouts remember November of that year and can probably tell you what they were doing on the 22nd. President Kennedy was assassinated and it became a punctuation mark for the 20th century.

I was biding my time until the opportunity arose to work with the Wellington Harbour Board, and it did within a few weeks. I then became a stevedore on Wellington's waterfront, often working with ex-seamen – some of whom I'd served with. There existed an edgy relationship between waterfront workers, who were heavily unionised, and employers going way back to 1951 when, depending on your point of view, there occurred a massive strike or lockout, which was declared a National Emergency. The work was steady but casual work and well paid too. If you wanted a day off you just rang in before 8 o'clock to tell them you weren't available, no sweat and no feeling that you were letting anyone down.

The work itself was of course manual but not too hard. We worked in gangs, either on the wharf or down the hatch of a vessel, following directions from the hatch man above who would co-ordinate our actions with the crane driver. There were often disputes settled between a union delegate and a rep from the Harbour Board. Perhaps an extra sixpence an hour for unloading dirty or smelly cargo would be demanded, or if someone spotted a mouse down below, the call would go out for 'Mouse-money'.

Attending union meetings and influenced by my workmates I began to become politicized, joined Wellington Public Library and took out books of a radical nature: Tressel's *Ragged Trousered Philanthropists* and Upton Sinclair's *The Jungle*, before I added Steinbeck, Howard Fast and Jack London to my reading list.

I got to know Peter Dukes, another ex-seaman as we worked together down on Aotea Quay, and we became buddies, even shared a flat together. We then got to know Dave Oppler, who worked in the T&G Insurance Offices and would always play the Devil's advocate when discussing anything serious. Alex Richardson was a Pom who worked in the Electronics Lab up at the University of Victoria. Peter Webb, another water-sider, who came from Tamworth in Australia, became another pal. So too did Jack Foshko, and because Jack was an older guy out of Greenwich Village, we accorded him respect. Suddenly I had a diverse group of mates, along with old and favourite ones like Johnny Murray and Johnny Bull, both of whom ended up living in

Wellington during the mid sixties. A small group of us got involved in something called 'The School of Economic Science'. We would religiously follow exercises based on the writings of Gurdjieff that were designed to focus the mind by being here, now and in the present. It was stimulating stuff for those of us who attempted to be intellectuals, and we'd find ourselves in The Green Door Coffee bar listening to Joan Baez as we discussed the meaning of life. To hear Jack Foshko and Dave Oppler, who had digested many esoteric books between them (*Zen and the Art of Motorcycle Maintenance*, *The Cosmic Consciousness* and stuff by Teilhard de Chardin), alluding to such books would have Dukesy and me, posing and puffing away at our pipes and listening with serious intent, ready at a moment to take up and challenge Jack and Dave, these two giants of erudition.

Foshko was of course quite ready to be mischievous and at a time when we were all prattling away, putting forth our take about dialectic materialism or Su Baba, he would slowly stir his coffee, allowing the tinkle of his spoon within the cup to summon us. Our prattling would halt as we respectfully allowed Jack a moment to make an observation. He would look up, knowing he had our attention, and say mildly, 'Y'know...when you add it all up, do the math, then think about it...life's nothing more than a cup of cawffee.' There'd then be whispers around the table.

'What'd he say?'

'Huh?'

'He said that life is like a what?' There'd be a moment whilst we grappled with his simile. We'd digest this pearl of great price with sober nods, waiting and hoping for enlightenment.

'Yeah Man!'

'Wow!'

'Far out!'

'Out-a-sight!'

But then brave Dukesy would challenge this and ask 'Can you unpack that, Jack? Life's like a cup of coffee, how so?'

Jack would then look to each of us and slowly say, 'Fucked if I know. I'm no god-damned philosopher.' We'd then drown out Baez or Dylan with great hoots of laughter. It was this ability not to take ourselves too seriously and realise that we were nothing but posers and 'up ourselves', and to know that the questions we asked were and would always be unknowable, that bonded us. The sound of one hand clapping!

***

I took a job as a postman after leaving the waterfront so that I could attend English literature lectures at the University of Wellington. I walked the Wellington hills, made friends with the dogs and got to know James K. Baxter, as I learnt his round. Jim at that time was embarked on his *'Pig Island Letters'* and was another 'one-off' who went on to become New Zealand's most famous poet. I remember him as a laid back man, always ready to look at housewives' poems and perhaps suggest improvements. Retired personnel from the Central Post Office probably remember him, too, as occasionally the phone would ring in the sorting office and a concerned housewife would be on the line.

'Hello! Mrs Crocker here in Brooklyn Terrace. Jim's asleep under a tree on my front lawn, should I wake him?'

'No, but thanks for your call, we wondered where he is, he'll be okay though, let him sleep it off.' Everybody during those times seemed prepared to cut each other some slack. Such happy days!

In 1966 I married a fine woman called Mary McLeary. She had emigrated from Birmingham and was - as Alex said - a slice of wholemeal bread. I had by then been in Wellington nearly three years and had made lots of new friends. Mary and I were married in St Paul's Cathedral and took our honeymoon on Akaroa Island. On our return we went to live in an old sheep station along the Happy Valley Road. I now had to think about a career and decided to train as a land surveyor part-time in the evenings at the local polytechnic. A late start at age 29 maybe, but Max Gandar & Son agreed to take me on as a chainman. I would travel to locations outside the city boundary with Ross Gandar and with machete, chain and theodolite help carve out sections of land, which then were plotted onto maps obtained from the Land Registry. I really liked the work as it involved both brain and brawn. Some days would find me hacking bush in vest, shorts and boots. Then at other times I'd be in the office using trigonometry, chain readings and temperature checks to calculate precise measurements and draw up scaled charts from field notes.

Mary was great and accepted my minimal training and unskilled wage. She worked as a shorthand typist for a government office and had left behind in Kings Heath her mum, dad and younger sister Celia. An older sister Elizabeth had gone to live in Germany with her new husband Hans. On an impulse I booked Mary a homeward voyage on the *Angelina Lauro* so that she could see Celia get married to one Michael Feeney. I think Mary had mixed feelings about my impulsive behaviour, but I was intending to return to Britain as well.

My plan was to present myself to the Wellington office of the Shaw Savill Company to apply to work my own passage home and then join Mary in Birmingham. There were many vacancies because so many seamen were jumping ship and I had no problem. I joined the *Gothic* on 12th June 1967 in Bluff (located at the bottom of the South island) as a hospital attendant and doctor's steward, arriving back in the Victoria Docks on 18th July, one month before my 30th birthday. This would be my last sea voyage.

Reflections

Now at its end, this memoir has been a major cathartic experience for me, helping to make sense of what continues to be a life full of personal shipwrecks and paradise islands. It's been my own *Desert Island Discs*. Before closing, however, I'd like to add a few words about the British Merchant Navy. The late 1950s were just about its final glory years. It still exists, but only as a shadow of its former self: no longer a national institution, it's been privatized, and the shipping companies run things on their own. They offer training places and careers to young men and women on ferries, cruise liners and a small number of bulk carriers.

At the time I first went to sea, in 1955, there were over two thousand British-registered ships steaming in and out of British ports every year, providing employment for millions. Who could have known? I didn't at the time, but the winds of trade, although still strong, were about to veer and the Red Ensign, the flag affectionately known as the Red Duster, would eventually lose its snapple and crack.

For those of my generation – I was born in 1937 – it was a fact that the sun never set on the British Empire. The lands throughout the globe that belonged to Great Britain were coloured red in my school atlas and our Merchant Navy had expanded to match Britain's imperial expansion. After World War II and the coming of independence for our former colonies, trade by British shipping began its slow decline. Then as early as April 1956 a purpose- built ship designed to hold containers, the SS *Ideal*, sailed from Port Newark in New Jersey to the Port of Houston, Texas. It might have been a ripple on a pond for all the publicity that it generated but Containerization, with a big C, had begun. Within little more than a decade, large working crews on board ship and dockside would no longer be needed, a revolution was under way. Liverpool and London, Bristol and Plymouth, Southampton and Hull, and many other ports that had provided employment for centuries would begin to diminish. Official figures reveal that by 1972 there were only 180 British-registered ships.

Industrial and economic progress cannot be stopped; the Luddites had found that out, and with the decline of the docks our shipbuilding industry also became a casualty. In a few years the old docks all fell silent and the skippers of vessels that were registered elsewhere set their course for Felixstowe, where facilities for containerized cargo had belatedly been built. Shipbuilding, which had once symbolized Britain's industrial might, had become eclipsed by the rise of Japanese and Korean companies and a new generation of container ships and tankers were built by those companies at half the price and in half the time. By the late 1980s British yards had only one order on their books at any one time. The Northeast's greatest yard, Swan Hunter, a shipbuilding site for 140 years, closed in 2009.

Another factor was air travel, of course, which in real terms had become cheaper during the 1960s. It had taken me 30 days to travel from London to New Zealand via the Panama Canal back in my years as a seaman. Now the modern jet plane meant that Sydney or Auckland were no more than a doze and a day away.

The once proud Red Duster drooped in the doldrums, and alternatives to life at sea had to be found by many. Maybe that was a good thing for some seafarers. 'Stay in too long and it'll destroy you for any other life,' the old adage advised, and yes, there was something to that. But I still count myself and others of my generation extremely lucky that we had a chance to realize our dreams and see the world.

BV - #0113 - 080424 - C2 - 210/148/21 - PB - 9781780356723 - Gloss Lamination